"Few people reading [barcode] lebt they owe to the mai who know the name of the fountainhead of modern English Bible translation, few realize that Tyndale fervently stood for the doctrines of justification by faith alone and salvation by grace alone. This little gem of a book reveals Tyndale's labors for the truth, his sufferings for the truth, and his love for the truth. May God use Steven Lawson's book to cause such love to burn in many others."

—DR. JOEL R. BEEKE
President, Puritan Reformed Theological Seminary
Grand Rapids, Mich.

"Much more than a biography, this thrilling chronicle quickens the Christian heart and stokes the fires of resolve to courageously defend and proclaim the truth. Dr. Lawson's diligent work on William Tyndale should be considered essential reading for every English-speaking believer, as it carefully unfolds the forgotten legacy of God's faithfulness in using one man, against all odds, to bring us the gospel in the English language."

—DAVID PARSONS
Founder, Truth Remains
Granada Hills, Calif.

"In the history of the Christian faith among English-speaking peoples, it was William Tyndale's translation of the Bible that made of them a people of the Book. His life was poured out even to the point of death to achieve this goal, and every generation of believers needs to hear the story of his life and death afresh. And one of the best guides to his story and its lessons for our day is this new study by Steve Lawson. Highly recommended!"

—DR. MICHAEL A.G. HAYKIN
Professor of church history and biblical spirituality
The Southern Baptist Theological Seminary
Louisville, Ky.

The Daring Mission of
William Tyndale

The Daring Mission of William Tyndale

STEVEN J. LAWSON

 LIGONIER MINISTRIES

The Daring Mission of William Tyndale
© 2015 by Steven J. Lawson

Published by Ligonier Ministries
421 Ligonier Court, Sanford, FL 32771
Ligonier.org

Printed in Ann Arbor, Michigan
Cushing-Malloy, Inc.
0001223
First edition, first paperback printing

ISBN 978-1-64289-568-1 (Paperback)
ISBN 978-1-56769-435-2 (Hardcover)
ISBN 978-1-64289-569-8 (ePub)

Cover design: Metaleap Creative
Interior design and typeset: Katherine Lloyd, The DESK

The Library of Congress has cataloged the Reformation Trust edition as follows:

Lawson, Steven J.
   The daring mission of William Tyndale / Steven J. Lawson. -- First edition.
      pages cm. -- (A long line of godly men profile)
   Includes bibliographical references and index.
   ISBN 978-1-56769-435-2 -- ISBN 1-56769-435-7
   1. Tyndale, William, -1536. 2. Reformation--England--Biography. 3. Bible.
      English--Versions--History--16th century. I. Title.
   BR350.T8L39 2015
   270.6092--dc23
   [B]   2014036617

This book is dedicated
to a faithful friend,
David Parsons,
a man who shares my passion and zeal
for the written Word of God
and its chief English translator and heroic martyr,
William Tyndale

Contents

Foreword

Followers Worthy to Be Followed

D own through the centuries, God has raised up a long line of godly men whom He has used mightily at strategic moments in church history. These valiant individuals have come from all walks of life, from the ivy-covered halls of elite schools to the dusty back rooms of tradesmen's shops. They have arisen from all points of this world, from highly visible venues in densely populated cities to obscure hamlets in remote places. Yet despite these differences, these pivotal figures have had much in common.

First and foremost, each man possessed an unwavering faith in the Lord Jesus Christ. But more can be said about these luminous figures. Each of these stalwarts of the faith also held deep convictions in the God-exalting truths known as the doctrines of grace. Though they differed in secondary matters of theology, they stood shoulder to shoulder in embracing these biblical teachings that magnify the sovereign grace of God in salvation. These spiritual leaders upheld the foundational truth that "salvation is of the Lord."[1]

---

1   Ps. 3:8; Jonah 2:9.

The doctrines of grace humbled their souls before God and kindled their hearts with greater passion for God. These truths of divine sovereignty emboldened these men to rise up and advance the cause of Christ in their generation. Any survey of redemptive history reveals that those who embrace these core Reformed truths are granted larger measures of confidence in their God. With an enlarged vision for the expanse of His kingdom upon the earth, they stepped forward boldly to accomplish the work of ten, twenty, even thirty men. These luminous individuals arose with wings like eagles and soared above their times. The doctrines of grace empowered them to serve God in their divinely appointed hour of history, leaving a godly inheritance for future generations to come.

This Long Line of Godly Men Profiles series highlights key figures in the agelong procession of these sovereign-grace men. The purpose of this series is to explore how these figures used their God-given gifts and abilities to impact their times and further the kingdom of heaven. Because they were courageous followers of Christ, their examples are worthy of emulation today.

This volume focuses upon the man regarded as the father of the English Bible, William Tyndale. In the sixteenth century, Tyndale forsook his native land of England and traveled to Europe in order to translate the Bible into the language of his countrymen. In an hour marked with great spiritual darkness, and at the cost of his own life, Tyndale courageously gave the English-speaking world a Bible they could read and understand. Perhaps no other Englishman has ever been used to affect the spiritual lives of so many people for so many centuries. William Tyndale stands as a towering figure, eminently worthy to be profiled in this series. Never have so many owed so much to so singular an effort.

May the Lord use this book to embolden a new generation of believers to bring its witness for Jesus Christ upon this world. Through this profile of Tyndale, may you be strengthened to walk in a manner worthy of your calling. May you be zealous in your study of the written Word of God for the exaltation of Christ and the advance of His kingdom.

Soli Deo gloria!

—Steven J. Lawson
Series editor

Father of
the English Bible

*Every true progress in church history is conditioned by
a new and deeper study of the Scriptures. . . . While the Humanists
went back to the ancient classics and revived the spirit of Greek and
Roman paganism, the Reformers went back to
the sacred Scriptures in the original languages and revived
the spirit of apostolic Christianity.*[1]

—PHILIP SCHAFF

F eatured prominently in my study, as though looking over my right shoulder, is a reproduction of a stunning portrait of the great Bible translator William Tyndale. Painted in oil on canvas, the original work is from the brush of an unknown artist. It was produced in the late seventeenth or early eighteenth century and now

---

1   Philip Schaff, *History of the Christian Church,* vol. 7 (1888; repr., Peabody, Mass.: Hendrickson, 2006), 1.

hangs in the National Portrait Gallery in London.[2] As the subject of the portrait, Tyndale is seated, dressed all in black, and surrounded by a subdued dark-brown background. His face and hands seem to glow from the light of a candle that is hidden from view.

Tyndale's left hand is balancing a book, keeping it horizontal lest it fall. This book is a Bible, the collection of divinely inspired writings that Tyndale devoted his life to translating from the Hebrew and Greek into English. His right hand appears to be resting on a dark table, while his right index finger is pointing emphatically to the Bible. Tyndale is directing the observer's attention away from himself, and instead drawing every eye toward this sacred Book in which he resolutely believed and to which he dedicated his whole life.

Beneath the Bible, the artist has painted an unfurled banner, seemingly suspended in air. Signifying Tyndale as an Oxford and Cambridge scholar, the writing on the banner is in Latin: *Hac ut luce tuas dispergam Roma tenebras sponte extorris ero sponte sacrificium.* This means, "To scatter Roman darkness by this light, the loss of land and life I will reckon slight." This bold message represents the life's mission of Tyndale. By translating the Bible into English, this brilliant linguist ignited the flame that would banish the spiritual darkness in England. Tyndale's translation of the Scriptures unveiled the divine light of biblical truth that would shine across the English-speaking world, ushering in the dawning of a new day.

In the background of this portrait, behind Tyndale, are the words *Gulielmus Tindilus Martyr.* This is the Latin rendering of

---

2   One of the most recognizable and famous portraits of William Tyndale hangs in the dining hall of Hertford College, Oxford University. The portrait to which I am referring is now part of the primary collection of the National Portrait Gallery, London.

this scholar's first and last name, along with the word *martyr,* which identifies the high cost paid by Tyndale to bring the Scriptures into the language of his countrymen. This heroic figure died a martyr's death in 1536, strangled to death by an iron chain, after which his corpse was burned and blown up by gunpowder that had been spread around his incinerated body.

At the bottom of the portrait, there is a panel giving the explanation of Tyndale's martyrdom. The words are in Latin and translate as follows:

> This picture represents, as far as art could, William Tyndale, sometime student of this Hall [Magdalen] and its ornament, who after establishing here the happy beginnings of a purer theology, at Antwerp devoted his energies to translating into the vernacular the New Testament and the Pentateuch, a labour so greatly tending to the salvation of his fellow-countrymen that he was rightly called the Apostle of England. He gained his martyr's crown at Vilvoorde near Brussels in 1536, a man, if we may believe even his adversary (the Emperor's Procurator General), learned, pious, and good.

The irony of this portrait is that Tyndale never sat for such a rendering. To protect his anonymity, he could not have his facial likeness reproduced onto canvas. The work he carried out came at too high a price to allow himself to be recognized. Only after his gruesome death could Tyndale be known.

This portrait of Tyndale hangs in my study as a constant visual reminder of the invaluable treasure that sits on my desk: the English Bible. It underscores the fact that as I preach its truths, spiritual light is being sent forth into this dark world. Moreover, this portrait bears witness to me of the great price required to unveil its truth in this sin-blackened age.

As Tyndale entered the world scene, England lay covered under a dark night of spiritual darkness. The church in England remained shrouded in the midnight of spiritual ignorance. The knowledge of the Scriptures had been all but extinguished in the land. Although there were some twenty thousand priests in England, it was said that they could not so much as translate into English a simple clause from the *Pater noster*—the Lord's Prayer. The clergy were so bogged down in a mire of religious superstition that they had no knowledge of the truth. The only English Scriptures were a few hand-copied Wycliffe Bibles, translated from the Latin Vulgate at the end of the fourteenth century. The Lollards, a small band of courageous preachers and followers of Wycliffe, unlawfully distributed these banned books. The mere possession of Wycliffe's translation led many to suffer. Some even faced death.

In 1401, Parliament passed legislation known as the *De haeretico comburendo*, which, as its title indicates, legalized the burning of heretics at the stake. Because of the perceived threat of the Lollards, translating the Bible into English was considered a capital crime. In 1408, Thomas Arundel, the archbishop of Canterbury, wrote the Constitutions of Oxford, forbidding any translation of the Bible into English unless authorized by the bishops:

> It is a dangerous thing . . . to translate the text of the Holy Scripture out of one tongue into another, for in the translation the same sense is not always easily kept. . . . We therefore decree and ordain, that no man hereafter, by his own authority translate any

text of the Scripture into English or any other tongue. . . . No man can read any such book . . . in part or in whole.[3]

Even teaching the Bible unlawfully in English was considered a crime worthy of death. In 1519, seven Lollards were burned at the stake for teaching their children the Lord's Prayer in English. A spiritual night had fallen over the land of England. The darkness that covered her could not have been any more stark.

At the same time, the Reformation fires were igniting places such as Wittenberg and Zürich and could not be contained. Sparks of divine truth soon leapt across the English Channel and ignited the dry tinder in England. By 1520, the works of Luther were being read and discussed by scholars in Oxford and Cambridge. Fanning this flame was the availability of Erasmus' Greek New Testament with his companion Latin translation that had been compiled in 1516, one year before Luther posted his Ninety-Five Theses. This resource was of great value to scholars, who read Greek and Latin. But it was of no use to the common Englishman, who could not read either language. If the Reformation were to come to England, it would not be enough to merely cry *sola Scriptura*. There must be the translation of the Bible into the English language for the people to read. But how would this ever come about?

In this dark hour, God raised up William Tyndale, an unmatched individual who possessed extraordinary linguistic skills combined with an unwavering devotion to the Bible. He was a remarkable scholar, proficient in eight languages—Hebrew, Greek, Latin, Italian,

---

3   Brian Moynahan, *God's Bestseller: William Tyndale, Thomas More, and the Writing of the English Bible; A Story of Martyrdom and Betrayal* (New York: St. Martin's, 2002), 1.

Spanish, English, German, and French. He possessed an unsurpassed ability to work with the sounds, rhythms, and senses of the English language. But in order to do his translation work, he would be forced to leave his native England, never to return. This resilient figure would live underground as a condemned heretic and hunted fugitive for the last twelve years of his life. He would eventually pay the ultimate price in giving his life unto a martyr's death to provide his countrymen with the New Testament and half of the Old Testament in English. His feat of translating the Bible into English from the original Greek and Hebrew had never before been accomplished. This remarkable Reformer would become the most significant of the early English Protestants.

It is this man, William Tyndale, whom we will consider in this small volume. Here is a man who gave the English-speaking people the Bible in their own language. May he be always esteemed as the one who first made the Scripture an accessible book to the common person in English.

Before we proceed any further, I want to thank the publishing team at Ligonier Ministries for their commitment to this Long Line of Godly Men Profiles series. I remain thankful for the ongoing influence of my former professor and current friend, Dr. R.C. Sproul. I must also express my gratitude to Chris Larson, who is so instrumental in overseeing this series.

Moreover, I am indebted to Christ Fellowship Baptist Church of Mobile, Ala., which I have served as senior pastor for more than eleven years. No pastor has ever been given as much encouragement to serve Christ on such a far-reaching scale as I have. I am extremely grateful for the support of my fellow elders and congregation, who have continuously encouraged me in my extended ministry abroad.

I want to express my gratitude for my executive ministry assistant, Kay Allen, who typed this document, and Dustin Benge, a fellow pastor at Christ Fellowship, who helped prepare this manuscript.

I thank God for my family who support me in my life and ministry. My wife, Anne, and our four children, Andrew, James, Grace Anne, and John, remain pillars of strength for me.

—Steven J. Lawson
Dallas
July 2014

1

A Dangerous
Passion

*The only true reformation is that which emanates from
the Word of God. The Holy Scriptures, by bearing witness
to the incarnation, death, and resurrection of the Son of God,
create in man by the Holy Ghost a faith which justifies him.*[1]

—J.H. MERLE D'AUBIGNÉ

William Tyndale, by translating the Bible from the Greek and Hebrew, became the "true father of the English Bible"[2] and launched a global influence for the spread of God's Word, extending to the present day. He likewise became the father of the English Reformation, as well as the father of the Modern English language. This monumental task of rendering the Bible from its original tongues gave rise to the Protestant movement in England and effected the standardization of the language of Modern English. Simply put,

---

1 J.H. Merle d'Aubigné, *The Reformation in England* (Edinburgh, Scotland: Banner of Truth, 1853, 1994), 1:167.
2 Sir Frederick Kenyon, *Our Bible and the Ancient Manuscripts: Being a History of the Text and Its Translations* (Whitefish, Mont.: Kessinger, 2007), 211, 217.

Tyndale helped launch the English Reformation by giving the people of England a pure translation of Scripture in their native tongue.

Tyndale was a daring pioneer who blazed the trail for the Reformation in his homeland. Noted Reformation historian J.H. Merle d'Aubigné calls Tyndale "the mighty mainspring of the English Reformation."[3] That is to say, Tyndale set into motion the spread of the Reformation throughout England and beyond. Preeminent among Bible translators, Tyndale possessed "a linguistic genius whose expertise in multiple languages dazzled the scholarly world of his day."[4] According to Tyndale biographer Brian Edwards, Tyndale was "the heart of the Reformation in England." In fact, Edwards further exclaims, Tyndale *was* the Reformation in England."[5]

These respected men are not alone in their accolades for Tyndale. The famous martyrologist John Foxe lauded Tyndale as "the Apostle of England ... the most remarkable figure among the first generation of English Protestants."[6] Through his translation work, Tyndale is regarded as "the first of the Puritans, or at least their grandfather."[7] He became the driving force that reshaped and reconfigured the English language. Translating the Bible into accessible English for the common person, Tyndale is celebrated as the "prophet of the

---

3 D'Aubigné, *The Reformation in England,* 1:167.
4 Leland Ryken, *The Word of God in English: Criteria for Excellence in Bible Translation* (Wheaton, Ill.: Crossway, 2002), 48.
5 Brian H. Edwards, *God's Outlaw: The Story of William Tyndale and the English Bible* (Darlington, England: Evangelical, 1976, 1999), 170. Italics original.
6 John Foxe, *Foxe's Book of Martyrs* (Nashville, Tenn.: Thomas Nelson, 2000), 114.
7 Robert Sheehan, "William Tyndale's Legacy," *The Banner of Truth* 24, no. 557, February 2010, 24.

English language."[8] Tyndale took supreme command of the Hebrew and Greek Scriptures and placed them into the hands of ordinary people in a readable English Bible.

With such lofty praise attached to Tyndale, certain questions need to be addressed for his place in the broader scope of church history to be fully appreciated. What steps did this chief architect of the English Bible take in order to produce his magnificent translation from the original languages? What challenges did he have to overcome in order to present this extraordinary gift to the English-speaking world? What high price did Tyndale ultimately pay in order to accomplish this extraordinary feat?

Before addressing these pertinent questions, we first want to address William Tyndale the man. Who was this luminous figure? What was the larger narrative of his life? Where did he carry out this history-altering task? It is to these questions that we will first devote ourselves.

Early Life and Studies

William Tyndale was born in the early 1490s, probably between 1493 and 1495, most likely in 1494. His family lived in rural western England, in the Slymbridge area of Gloucestershire near the Welsh border and Severn River. During the Wars of the Roses in the fifteenth century, Tyndale's ancestors migrated to the Gloucestershire area and became landowners. Tyndale was placed by God into a industrious family of respectable farmers who made their livelihood by cultivating their land. The Tyndale family was reasonably successful, flourishing in one of the most prosperous counties in England.

---

8   Ibid., 29.

This relative prosperity allowed William's parents to send him to Oxford, England's most prestigious university.

Little is known about William's younger years, which remain shrouded in obscurity. What is known, however, is that Tyndale had at least two brothers, Edward and John. Like their father, his brother John became an able and successful land manager who oversaw their Gloucestershire farm. The other brother, Edward, became a crown steward in Gloucestershire, who received rent for the use of Berkeley land for the king. In future years, William would exert a direct influence upon his brothers for the cause of the Reformation in England. As a result, John would be fined for possessing and distributing Bibles, a serious crime at the time in England. Upon his death, Edward would leave a number of Reformed books in his last will and testament.

In 1506, at age 12, William entered Magdalen Hall, which was located inside Magdalen College and attached to Oxford University. He spent ten years, from 1506 to 1516, studying at Oxford.[9] In Magdalen Hall, Tyndale spent the first two years in the equivalence of a preparatory grammar school. There he studied grammar, arithmetic, geometry, astronomy, music theory, rhetoric, logic, and philosophy. Upon entering Oxford, he demonstrated great aptitude and progress in languages under the finest classical scholars. While there, Tyndale was ordained into the priesthood, though he never entered a monastic order.

After graduating with a bachelor of arts on July 4, 1512, Tyndale set his sights on a master's degree from Oxford. It was not until the

---

9   David Daniell, *William Tyndale: A Biography* (New Haven, Conn.: Yale University Press, 1994), 38.

late stage of his education, after eight or nine years, that he finally was allowed to study theology. However, it was only speculative theology, with priority given to Aristotle and other Greek philosophers rather than the Bible. Upon reflection, Tyndale expressed his great disappointment with being shielded from the Bible and theology:

> In the universities, they have ordained that no man shall look on the Scripture until he be noselled [nursed] in heathen learning eight or nine years, and armed with false principles with which he is clean shut out of the understanding of the Scripture. ... [T]he Scripture is locked up with ... false expositions, and with false principles of natural philosophy.[10]

Such a spiritually impoverished education hindered Tyndale from knowing the truth of Scripture. In July 1515, Tyndale graduated with a master of arts as a university-trained linguist from the highly acclaimed Oxford University. Little is known about what Tyndale chose to do immediately afterward. There is consensus that he likely pursued further studies at Oxford and gave classroom instruction there.

In 1519, Tyndale went to study at Cambridge, regarded as "Oxford's foremost intellectual rival in England."[11] Scholars suggest that he may have received a degree while there.[12] Prior to Tyndale's

---

10 William Tyndale, "The Practice of Prelates," *The Works of William Tyndale* (1849 and 1850; repr., Edinburgh, Scotland: Banner of Truth, 2010), 2:291.

11 Alister E. McGrath, *In the Beginning: The Story of the King James Bible and How It Changed a Nation, a Language, and a Culture* (New York: Doubleday, 2001), 68.

12 Daniell writes that the time Tyndale spent at Cambridge may have been "short or longer, between 1517 and 1521." *William Tyndale*, 49.

arrival, the famed Dutch Renaissance humanist Desiderius Erasmus of Rotterdam (1466–1536) lectured in Greek at Cambridge from 1511 to 1514. During Tyndale's time there, Erasmus was traveling around Europe, compiling his famous Greek New Testament.

Cambridge had become a hotbed for the Protestant teaching of the German Reformer Martin Luther. Many of Luther's works were accessible at Cambridge, being broadly circulated among instructors and students alike. This exposure generated a building excitement on campus as these truths captivated many brilliant minds. As such, Cambridge was becoming the training ground for future reformers and martyrs. Under this influence of the Bible, Tyndale embraced a deep commitment to the core truths of the Protestant movement.

In 1520, a small group of Cambridge scholars began meeting regularly to discuss this new theology. A mere three years earlier, Luther had posted his Ninety-Five Theses in Wittenberg, Germany, on October 31, 1517. These truth-seeking students gathered at a local pub on the campus of King's College, called the White Horse Inn, to debate the ideas of Luther. This group became known as "Little Germany." In this small circle were many future leaders in the Reformed movement in England. These included Robert Barnes, Nicholas Ridley, Hugh Latimer, Miles Coverdale, Thomas Cranmer, Thomas Bilney, and, many believe, William Tyndale.[13] Of this group, two became archbishops, seven became bishops, and eight would be Protestant martyrs—Bilney, Tyndale, Clark, Frith, Lambert, Barnes, Ridley, and Latimer. These informal gatherings became

---

13 Some historians, including Brian H. Edwards and S.M. Houghton, assert that William Tyndale was in all probability at the White Horse Inn. Others, like Daniell, think Tyndale was not present.

the kindling for the English Reformation that would soon spread like wildfire across the British Isles.

Birthing a Vision

In 1521, Tyndale came to the conclusion that he needed to step away from the academic atmosphere in order to give more careful thought to the truths of the Reformation. Specifically, this young scholar wanted time to study and digest the Greek New Testament. He took a job in Gloucestershire, less than twelve miles from his birthplace, working for the wealthy family of Sir John Walsh at their estate, Little Sodbury. Tyndale served as the primary tutor for the children, private chaplain for the family, and personal secretary to Sir John. During this period, he preached regularly to a little congregation in nearby St. Adeline.

In considering the spiritual state of England, Tyndale came to the sober realization that England would never be evangelized using Latin Bibles. He concluded, "It was impossible to establish the lay people in any truth, except the Scripture were laid before their eyes in their mother tongue."[14] As he traveled throughout the region, fulfilling opportunities to preach, his beliefs were becoming well known as being distinctly Luther-like. His convictions became so strong that he found himself in disputes with officials in the Roman Catholic Church over the nature of the true gospel. Around 1522, Tyndale was called before John Bell, the chancellor of Worcester, and warned about his controversial views. No formal charges were leveled against him at the time, but this conflict was a foretaste of what was to come.

---

14 William Tyndale, "The Preface of Master William Tyndale, That He Made Before the Five Books of Moses, Called Genesis," in *The Works of William Tyndale* (1848; repr., Edinburgh, Scotland: Banner of Truth, 2010), 394.

As local priests came to dine at the Walsh manor, Tyndale witnessed firsthand the appalling biblical ignorance of the Roman church. During one meal, he found himself in a heated debate with a Catholic clergyman. The priest asserted, "We had better be without God's law than the pope's."[15] Tyndale boldly responded, "I defy the pope and all his laws." He then added that "if God spared him life, ere many years he would cause a boy that drives the plough to know more of the Scripture than he does."[16] Tyndale was echoing Erasmus' words in the preface to his recently published Greek New Testament: "I would to God that the plowman would sing a text of the Scripture at his plow and that the weaver would hum them to the tune of his shuttle."[17] From this point forward, the ambitious task of translating the Bible into English was the dominating pursuit of his life.

Tyndale traveled to London in 1523 to seek official authorization for a sanctioned translation and publication of an English Bible. He arranged a meeting with the bishop of London, Cuthbert Tunstall, a scholarly man and well-known classicist who had worked with Erasmus on the latter's Greek New Testament. Because of this association with Erasmus, Tyndale presumed Tunstall would be open to his translation project. Instead, Tyndale met great resistance to the idea of an English translation. Tunstall became highly suspicious of Tyndale's theology, which he feared would spread Luther's Protestant doctrines and lead to an upheaval in England such as was occurring in Germany. Luther's newly translated German Bible, released in September 1522, had thrown the region of Saxony into

15 *Foxe's Book of Martyrs*, 1:77.
16 "Biographical Notice of William Tyndale," in *Works,* 1:xix.
17 Erasmus as quoted in Philip Schaff, *History of the Christian Church* (1858; repr., Peabody, Mass.: Hendrickson, 2006), 6:724.

turmoil. Tunstall believed that a Bible in English, accessible to the people, would produce much the same mayhem in England, and so he stonewalled Tyndale.

But this tactic only deepened Tyndale's convictions that England desperately needed a Bible that the common man could read. The only question was how or where it could be done.

While in London, Tyndale preached numerous times at St. Dunstan's Church. One day, a wealthy cloth merchant named Humphrey Monmouth heard Tyndale preach at St. Dunstan's and decided to underwrite his expenses. This benefactor allowed Tyndale to remain in London for one year as he developed a plan for his Bible translation.

That plan involved a radical move. If Tyndale was to accomplish his daring mission, he realized, "There was no place to do it in all England."[18] Opposed by both the English church and crown, Tyndale realized he must leave the country and undertake his epic work elsewhere.

In the spring of 1524, at age 30, Tyndale sailed to the European Continent to launch his translation and publishing endeavor. He would do so without the king of England's consent, a clear breach of the established law. As a result, every biblical text he translated, he translated illegally. When he departed his native shores, Tyndale lived in exile for the remainder of his life. Never again would he return to his beloved homeland. For the next twelve years, Tyndale would live on foreign soil as a fugitive and outlaw of the English crown.

---

18 *Works,* 1:xxii.

The Work Begins

Arriving first in Hamburg, Germany, in 1524, Tyndale soon journeyed to Wittenberg to sit under the great German Reformer Martin Luther. He may have done so incognito. British scholar Tony Lane writes:

> It appears that he first went to Wittenberg to study. Contemporaries such as Thomas More refer to his time there. There is also an entry in the matriculation register for 27 May 1524 reading "Guillelmus Daltici Ex Angelia." If the final "ci" is a copyist's error for "n" we have an anagram of "Tindal" with the two syllables reversed.[19]

If this is, indeed, the name William Tyndale listed on the matriculation register in Wittenberg, he would have met Luther. This encounter would have come at a time when the German Reformer had thrown off the last vestiges of popish allegiance.[20] Such an influence upon Tyndale would have been significant.

While in Wittenberg, Tyndale began the work of translating the New Testament from Greek into English. It appears he undertook a major portion of this work from May to July 1525. The impact of Philip Melanchthon, a master of the Greek language, would have also been invaluable.

Accompanied by his amanuensis, Tyndale traveled to Cologne, the most populous city in Germany, in August 1525, where he

---

19 A.N.S. Lane, "William Tyndale," in *Biographical Dictionary of Evangelicals*, ed. Timothy Larsen (Downers Grove, Ill.: InterVarsity Press, 2003), 678.
20 John McClintock and James Strong, eds., *Cyclopedia of Biblical, Theological, and Ecclesiastical Literature,* vol. 10 (1867–87; repr., Grand Rapids, Mich.: Baker Academic, 1981), s.v. "William Tyndale."

completed his translation of the New Testament. In this bustling city, it was easy for the two Englishmen to be lost in the shuffle. Here, Tyndale found a printer, Peter Quentell, who agreed to print his new translation. However, the secrecy of the printing was breached when one of the print workers came under the influence of wine and spoke openly of the clandestine endeavor. John Cochlaeus, a bitter opponent of the Reformation, overheard talk of this forbidden project and immediately arranged for a raid on the print shop. Tyndale was forewarned and quickly gathered the few printed leaves along with the rest of his unprinted New Testament translation, escaping under the cover of night.

Fleeing down the Rhine River, Tyndale arrived in the more Protestant-friendly city of Worms in 1526. This was the very city where Luther had stood trial for heresy a mere five years before. Luther's teachings had exerted a strong influence on the city, making it sympathetic to the Protestant cause. Tyndale again found a printer, Peter Schoeffer, willing to publish his work.

Tyndale's New Testament was the first to be translated from the original Greek into English. Further, it was the first English Bible to be mechanically printed. Previously, there were only a few handwritten copies of John Wycliffe's Bible in English, translated a century and a half earlier. But Wycliffe's rendering was loosely translated from Latin, not Greek. Tyndale's work was far superior. Schoeffer completed the initial print run by producing some three thousand copies. Over the next eight years, two additional revised editions of Tyndale's New Testament would follow, as well as several pirated editions published by unauthorized printers.

Ready for delivery in the spring of 1526, Tyndale shipped his Bibles, hidden in bales of cotton, along the international trade routes to England. German Lutheran cloth merchants in England received the disguised shipment, ready to distribute the Bibles. Once past the royal agents, these forbidden books were picked up by a secret Protestant society, the Christian Brethren, and taken throughout England to various cities, universities, and monasteries. The newly printed Bibles were sold to eager Englishmen—merchants, students, tailors, weavers, bricklayers, and peasants alike—all hungry to read and grow in their knowledge of God's Word. Each New Testament cost three shillings and two pence, a week's wages for a skilled laborer—a remarkably affordable price for the average person.

By the summer of 1526, church officials in England had discovered this underground circulation of Tyndale's Bible. The archbishop of Canterbury and the bishop of London were enraged, and they confiscated every Tyndale Bible they could find. Church officials immediately declared the purchase, sale, distribution, or possession of this Bible a serious crime that would result in severe punishment. At St. Paul's Cross in London, Bishop Cuthbert Tunstall preached a scathing sermon against the Tyndale Bible and ceremonially burned copies of this unlawful volume. This demonstration sounded a public warning, though it hardly squelched the desire of the people to gain access to the Word of God in their own language.

Opposition and Obstacles

Tyndale's opponents in May 1527 hatched an ingenious plan to stop the spread of the unauthorized Bibles. William Warham, the archbishop of Canterbury, conspired to purchase the remaining copies of the Bible in order to destroy them. At first, this diabolical plot seemed brilliant. But it quickly backfired as the money from the sales provided the needed resources for Tyndale to then produce a revised second edition of his work. What Warham meant for evil, God meant for good. This allowed an even better version to be produced, with a larger print run.

Tyndale published his first major theological work, *The Parable of the Wicked Mammon*, in May 1528. This treatise focused on the very heart of the gospel, namely, justification by faith alone in Christ alone. Tyndale proclaimed that faith alone saves, and true faith produces a living obedience to God's Word. This significant work drew heavily upon Luther's works on this same subject. In places, Tyndale's writings are merely a translation or paraphrase of the German Reformer's own words. As hostility toward Tyndale grew, he disguised his location by having the name of a nonexistent printer—Hans Luft—printed on the title page, along with a false place of publication—Marburg, Germany. In reality, this important doctrinal work was printed by John Hoochstraten in the city of Antwerp.

Tyndale's opponents soon implemented a more aggressive plan to stop Tyndale. On June 18, 1528, an English cardinal, Thomas Wolsey, dispatched three agents to the Continent to search for Tyndale. Wolsey also ordered John Hacket, English ambassador to the Low Countries (modern-day Netherlands, Belgium, and Luxembourg), to demand that the regent authorize the arrest of Tyndale. A manhunt was launched for this notorious enemy of the state, and anyone who assisted him was to be punished. Still, all attempts to catch this elusive Reformer were unproductive, as he shrewdly withdrew to Marburg for safety. Hacket reported back to England that Tyndale was nowhere to be found.

While in Marburg, Tyndale penned a second title, *The Obedience of a Christian Man* (1528). Tyndale called upon every Christian to submit to every authority, including kings and magistrates. The existing hierarchy of the Catholic Church in England, he further claimed, possessed no real spiritual authority. When King Henry VIII read this work, he immediately approved its message, commenting, "This book is for me and all kings to read!"[21] Apart from his New Testament translation, *The Obedience of a Christian Man* is Tyndale's most influential work.

In September 1528, Tyndale's opponents made yet another serious attempt to track him down. A friar named John West was dispatched from England to the European Continent to find, seize, and bring this runaway Reformer back to England. West arrived in Antwerp, dressed in civilian attire, and began scouring cities and interrogating printers, searching for the stealthy translator. At the same time, Hermann Rinck, a Cologne senator, was buying and destroying all the Tyndale Bibles he could locate. Sensing the pressure, Tyndale remained undercover in Marburg, improving his ability in Hebrew, a language unknown in England. With this new skill in hand, Tyndale immediately set out to translate the Hebrew Old Testament into English, while continuing a careful revision of his New Testament.

To conceal his whereabouts, Tyndale shifted his location in 1529 from Marburg to Antwerp, then part of the Holy Roman Empire and now in modern-day Belgium. This thriving metropolis offered him access to capable printers, fellowship with reform-minded Englishmen, and a more direct shipping route to England. Here, Tyndale completed his translation of the five books of Moses.

With a new manhunt under way, Tyndale concluded that the danger was too great to remain in this large city. Realizing the Pentateuch

---

21 Robert Demaus and Richard Lovett, *William Tyndale: A Biography* (London: The Religious Tract Society, 1886), 205.

must be printed elsewhere, he boarded a ship in Antwerp, sailing to the mouth of the Elbe River in Germany. His plan was then to venture south to Hamburg. However, the voyage was halted by a severe storm, causing shipwreck off the coast of the Low Countries. Tragically, all his books, writings, and translation of the Pentateuch were lost. With unwavering determination, Tyndale was forced to undertake this enormous translation task yet again.

After enduring this devastating loss, Tyndale finally arrived in Hamburg. He was received into the house of the von Emerson family, who were strongly sympathetic to the cause of the Reformation. While there, Tyndale was reunited with Miles Coverdale, a Cambridge classmate. Coverdale would eventually complete his own translation of the Bible into English, though not from the original languages, and publish it in 1535 in what is known as the Coverdale Bible. In this cloistered environment, Tyndale undertook the laborious task of retranslating the Pentateuch from Hebrew into English. This arduous work, with Coverdale's assistance, took him from March to December 1529.

That same year, Sir Thomas More, the king's devout and intelligent lord chancellor, was commissioned by the king and the church in England to launch a character assassination upon Tyndale. The attack escalated with the publishing of *A Dialogue Concerning Heresies*, a vicious work in which More assaulted Tyndale, labeling him "the captain of English heretics," "a hell-hound in the kennel of the devil," "a new Judas," "worse than Sodom and Gomorrah," "an idolater and devil-worshipper," and "a beast out of whose brutish beastly mouth cometh a filthy foam."[22] More, a staunch enemy of the Reformation,

---

22 Thomas More, cited in N.R. Needham, *2000 Years of Christ's Power, Part 3: Renaissance and Reformation* (London: Grace, 2004), 381.

maintained that the Roman Catholic Church is the only true church. Whoever opposes the infallible teaching of Rome, he pronounced, is a heretic. This was a shot fired across Tyndale's bow. The English Reformer, by contrast, contended that trust must be placed in Scripture alone, not in the church. Anything short of this, Tyndale insisted, is of the spirit of antichrist.

Undeterred by the resistance from his homeland, Tyndale published the five books of Moses in January 1530 in Antwerp. Hoochstraten printed this small volume under the publishing pseudonym *Hans Luft at Marburg*. Like Tyndale's New Testament several years before, these books were smuggled into England and distributed. Tyndale's plans remained ambitious: to complete the translation of the entire Old Testament.

In late 1530, *The Practice of Prelates* appeared from the Reformer's pen. This work was a strong polemic against the Catholic clergy, documenting the corrupt relationship between the English crown and the papacy. As a result, this book transformed King Henry VIII into an avowed enemy of Tyndale.

Still another strategy was launched to apprehend Tyndale. In November 1530, Thomas Cromwell, an adviser to King Henry VIII, commissioned Stephen Vaughan, an English merchant sympathetic to the Reformed cause, to find Tyndale. Vaughan was instructed to offer Tyndale a salary and safe passage back to England. Upon his arrival on the Continent, Vaughan dispatched three letters to Tyndale, each addressed to three different cities—Frankfurt, Hamburg, and Marburg. Surprisingly, he received a response from Tyndale. As a result, a series of secret meetings were arranged in Antwerp in April 1531.

Vaughan attempted to persuade Tyndale to return to England. The tenacious translator agreed to return to England, but only on one condition. The king must choose someone else to translate the Bible into English. If Henry agreed, Tyndale would return to England, cease his translation work, and offer his life in service to the king. Similar promises of safety had been made earlier to John Hus and Luther but were broken. Tyndale knew the king's promise would not be kept.

Vaughan wrote from Antwerp on June 19 these simple words: "I find him [Tyndale] always singing one note."[23] In other words, Tyndale refused to change his tune. He would not promise to cease writing books or return to England until the king commissioned a Bible in the English language. Vaughan returned to England empty-handed. Tyndale was undaunted in his mission and could not be diverted from fulfilling this singular passion of his heart. In defiance of the English throne, he chose to continue his daring pursuit.

With attempts to apprehend Tyndale failing, Cromwell devised an even more aggressive strategy. Sir Thomas Elyot, a new emissary, was dispatched to Europe to apprehend Tyndale. His marching orders were to find Tyndale and bring him to the king, whatever it took. Elyot searched high and low, but his concerted effort yielded no positive results. Elyot returned to England without the despised renegade.

In 1531, Tyndale issued a treatise in response to the attacks in More's *Dialogue*, released in 1529. It was titled *Answer*; in it, he exegetically defended his translation of selected biblical passages that More claimed would lead people away from Roman Catholic theology and practice. Tyndale contended that Scripture was clear enough to be understood without church leadership imposing its twisted,

---

23 Daniell, *William Tyndale*, 217.

man-made tradition. More countered in 1532 and 1533 with his six-volume work *Confutation of Tyndale's Answer*. At nearly half a million words, the *Confutation* was the most imposing of More's polemical works, written as an imaginary dialogue between More and Tyndale with More addressing each of Tyndale's criticisms of Catholic rites and doctrines. These weighty tomes alleged that Tyndale was a traitor to England and a heretic. Despite More's vicious attack upon Tyndale, the Reformed cause was spreading across Europe and now England.

Betrayed, Imprisoned, and Condemned

In the early months of 1534, Tyndale moved into a house of English merchants in Antwerp as the guest of Thomas Poyntz, a wealthy English merchant. Sympathetic to the Reformed cause, Poyntz was "a good shrewd friend and loyal sympathizer."[24] He placed Tyndale under his protection, even providing a stipend as Tyndale worked on his translation project and other writings. The chaplain of this English house was a man named John Rogers. Through Tyndale's instruction and influence, Rogers became a loyal supporter of Reformed doctrines. Eventually, Rogers would compile his own English Bible in 1537, known as the Matthew Bible. This famous edition contained Tyndale's New Testament, Pentateuch, Historical Books, and Jonah, with minor changes. The rest of the Old Testament was drawn from the Coverdale Bible. In 1555, Rogers would become the first Protestant martyr under Queen Mary I, also known as "Bloody Mary."

Feeling more secure, Tyndale set himself to work on the revision of his New Testament translation, which has been called "the glory of

---

24 Ibid., 361.

his life's work."[25] This second edition appeared in 1534, eight years after the first. It contains some four thousand changes to the 1526 edition, though some claim it has as many as five thousand edits. These numerous corrections were the result of his further study of the original language and of feedback he received. A short prologue was placed before each New Testament book except Acts and Revelation. In addition, Tyndale added cross-references and explanatory notes to the biblical text in the outside margin, and marked off the literary units of each book on the inside margin. All six thousand printed copies of Tyndale's revised second edition of the New Testament sold out within a month.

A third edition would follow in December 1534 and early 1535, but with significantly fewer corrections. By this time, Tyndale's mastery of Hebrew was as advanced as his knowledge of Greek. This afforded him the ability to translate the next section of the Old Testament, Joshua through 2 Chronicles. This season of Tyndale's life proved to be extremely prolific. But all was about to change.

In England, a man named Henry Phillips found himself in a disastrous situation after gambling away a large sum of money his father had given him to pay a debt. A high official in the church, possibly the bishop of London, John Stokesley, became aware of his desperate plight. Phillips was viewed as a perfect accomplice for another devious strategy to arrest Tyndale. He was offered a large sum of money to travel to Europe and locate Tyndale. Like Judas, Phillips took the offer.

Phillips arrived in Antwerp in early summer of 1535. He made the necessary contacts among English merchants and followed the

---

25 Ibid., 316.

trail that led him straight to Tyndale. Phillips diabolically established a sham friendship with Tyndale. Despite the warning of Poyntz, Phillips secured Tyndale's trust and lured him into a narrow alley, where soldiers waited to arrest him.

After twelve years as a fugitive, the elusive Tyndale was at last apprehended and taken into custody. Upon his arrest, the bulky manuscript of his most recent translation work, Joshua to 2 Chronicles, escaped confiscation. It was likely Rogers, his close friend and companion, who gathered it up for safe possession. Rogers later took up Tyndale's cause and had his final work printed in the Matthew Bible.

Upon his capture, Tyndale was imprisoned six miles north of Brussels in the castle of Vilvoorde. With an imposing moat, seven towers, three drawbridges, and impenetrable walls, the castle was a fortress of confinement. Shivering in the cold, damp dungeons of this castle-prison, Tyndale waited more than a year for his trial, which was a mockery of justice. During his five-hundred-day confinement, Tyndale wrote another treatise, *Faith Alone Justifies before God*. To the end, Tyndale defended the seminal truth that lay behind his imprisonment.

During the harsh winter of 1535, Tyndale wrote in a final letter: "I suffer greatly from cold in the head, and am afflicted by a perpetual catarrh [discharge], which is much increase in this cell. . . . My overcoat is worn out; my shirts are also worn out." He requested "a lamp in the evening; it is indeed wearisome sitting alone in the dark. But most of all I beg and beseech your clemency to be urgent with the commissary . . . permit me to have my Hebrew Bible, Hebrew Grammar, and Hebrew Dictionary, that I may pass the time in that study."[26]

---

26 William Tyndale, introduction to *Tyndale's New Testament*, ed. and with an introduction by David Daniell (New Haven, Conn.: Yale University Press, 1989), ix.

These months were "a long dying leading to dying."[27] The martyrologist John Foxe wrote that as Tyndale sat in prison, he "was affecting his very . . . enemies" as "he converted his keeper, the keeper's daughter, and others of his household."[28] Though cold and suffering within the bowels of this stone prison, like the Apostle Paul in his Roman prison, Tyndale's heart was still ablaze with gospel truth and undeniable joy.

In August 1536, Tyndale stood trial before his accusers, who leveled a long list of charges against him. Among his offenses, Tyndale asserted that justification is by faith alone, human traditions cannot bind the conscience, the human will is bound by sin, there is no purgatory, neither Mary nor the saints offer prayers for us, and we are not to pray to them. All this made Tyndale an enemy of both church and state. He was condemned as a heretic.

During a public service, Tyndale would have been excommunicated and stripped of his priesthood. According to the custom for such ceremonies, Tyndale emerged before a large gathering wearing his priestly robes. He was forced to kneel, as his hands would be scraped with a knife or sharp glass, symbolizing the loss of all privileges of the priesthood. The bread and wine of the Mass would be placed into his hands and then removed. He would be stripped of his vestments and reclothed as a layman. He would then be delivered over to the civil authorities for the inevitable sentence to death. Forced back into his dungeon cell, a steady stream of priests and monks came to harass him and seek a recanting.

---

27 John Piper, *Filling Up the Afflictions of Christ: The Cost of Bringing the Gospel to the Nations in the Lives of William Tyndale, Adoniram Judson, and John Paton* (Wheaton, Ill.: Crossway, 2009), 50.

28 *Foxe's Book of Martyrs*, 127.

"Lord, Open the King's Eyes"

On October 6, 1536, Tyndale emerged from the castle and was paraded to the southern gate of the town, where his execution stake awaited. A large crowd assembled behind a barricade. In the middle of a circular space, two great beams were raised in the familiar form of a cross. Hanging from the top of the central beam was a strong iron chain. Brushwood, straw, and logs were bundled and piled at its base. Amid pomp and pharisaical splendor, the procurer-general and the great doctors took their seats as spectators. The massive crowd parted, allowing the guards to bring Tyndale closer to his execution.

Tyndale proceeded to the cross. The guards bound his feet to the bottom of the cross as the chain was fastened around his neck, pulling him tightly to the beam of wood. The wood was rearranged around the prisoner to encase him in combustible material. Gunpowder was sprinkled thoroughly on the brush. The executioner stood behind the cross, awaiting the signal from the procurer-general to carry out the sentence. It was likely at this moment that Tyndale gazed into the heavens and cried forth in prayer, "Lord, open the king of England's eyes."[29]

The procurer-general gave the signal and the executioner quickly tightened the iron noose, strangling Tyndale. The crowd watched Tyndale gasp for air as he suffocated and died. However, his mere death did not satisfy. The procurer-general grabbed a lighted wax torch and handed it to the executioner, who threw it on the straw and brushwood. The blazing fire caused the gunpowder to explode, blowing up the corpse. What remained of the limply hanging, burnt body of Tyndale fell into the raging fire.[30]

---

29 Ibid., 83.
30 This scene has been reconstructed by David Daniell from other similar capital punishments at the time of Tyndale. Daniell, *William Tyndale*, 383.

God ultimately answered Tyndale's dying prayer. In the year he was martyred, 1536, a complete English Bible was already circulating in England, unknown to Tyndale. This work was predominately drawn from Tyndale's own translation. The first of these Bibles was the Coverdale Bible, printed in 1535. A second English translation of the entire Bible would come as a result of the efforts of John Rogers in 1537. This version was known as the Matthew Bible.

Less than a year after Tyndale's death, Thomas Cranmer, who had become the archbishop of Canterbury, and Oliver Cromwell persuaded Henry VIII to approve the publication of an official English Bible. When King Henry saw the Coverdale Bible, he emphatically proclaimed, "If there be no heresies in it, then let it be spread abroad among all the people!"[31] In September 1538, the king issued a decree that a copy of the Bible in English and Latin should be placed in every church in England. The permissible copies of the Bible were the Coverdale Bible and the Matthew Bible, both flowing, in large measure, from the influence and pen of William Tyndale. In 1539, Coverdale issued a revised version of his translation called the Great Bible (so named for its large size), which received popular acclaim and the official approval of the king.

The historian J.H. Merle d'Aubigné writes that after Tyndale's death, the stream of English Bibles into England was "like a mighty river continually bearing new waters to the sea."[32] As these printed

---

31 William J. McRae, *A Book to Die For: A Practical Study Guide on How Our Bible Came to Us* (Toronto: Clements, 2002), xiv, cited in Tony Lane, "A Man for All People: Introducing William Tyndale," *Christian History* 6, no. 4 (1987), 6–9.

32 J.H. Merle d'Aubigné, *The Reformation in England* (1866–78; repr., Edinburgh, Scotland: Banner of Truth, 1994), 2:348.

English Bibles became accessible to the common man in England, Tyndale's plowman was, at last, reading, discussing, living, and proclaiming the truths of the Bible among his relatives, friends, and countrymen.

Almost five hundred years later, the river of Scripture continues to flow mightily across the face of the globe. Tyndale's translation and those based on it formed the basis of the King James Version in 1611, and through it, nearly every English translation since. Today, English translations are numerous, yet they have their singular origin in Tyndale's foundational work. Publishers of English Bibles continue to stand upon the sturdy shoulders of Tyndale's pioneering efforts. Given that English is an international language, the ongoing influence of William Tyndale extends to the farthest corners of the world.

As the current of truth surges forth in this present hour, may the truths of God's Word inundate our hearts and the swells of sovereign grace flood over our minds. May there be a renewed commitment to the sufficiency and exclusivity of this bloodstained Book.

2

Grounded in Sovereign Grace

Tyndale was more than a mildly theological thinker. He is at last
being understood as, theologically as well as linguistically, well
ahead of his time. For him, as decades later for Calvin, . . . the
overriding message of the New Testament is the sovereignty of God.
Everything is contained in that. It must never, as he wrote,
be lost from sight. . . . For Tyndale, God is, above all, sovereign,
active in the individual and in history.[1]

—DAVID DANIELL

Hailed as "the greatest of the early English Protestants,"[2] William Tyndale was a Reformer in every sense of the word. This certainly included his theology. Undergirding his belief in Reformation truth was his unwavering commitment to the sovereignty of God in the salvation of sinners. It was this deep confidence in the

---

1   David Daniell, introduction to William Tyndale, *Selected Writings*, ed. and
    with an introduction by David Daniell (New York: Routledge, 2003), viii–ix.
2   Needham, 378.

doctrines of grace that gave him staying power in his tireless efforts to translate the Bible into English. Tyndale was convinced that the power of God alone could change the hearts of kings and plowboys alike. The glorious truth that Christ would build His church compelled Tyndale to bring the Scriptures to the English people in their own language, regardless of the dangers he faced.

In the Protestant Reformation of the sixteenth century, the doctrines of sovereign grace provided a firm foundation for a host of Bible translators. In Germany in 1522, Martin Luther translated the New Testament into the language of his people. This German stalwart was equally known for being rooted and grounded in the fertile soil of sovereign grace. In the British Isles, the Englishmen Miles Coverdale and John Rogers produced the Coverdale Bible (1535) and the Matthew Bible (1537), respectively; each man was undergirded by a strong belief in divine sovereignty. In Switzerland, this same unflinching confidence in God's sovereignty in man's salvation burned brightly in the translators of the Geneva Bible (1560), including John Knox of Scotland. Geneva became virtually synonymous with the truth of sovereign election. In England, a century and a half before Tyndale, John Wycliffe translated the Bible into English from the Latin Vulgate. This Oxford professor likewise held firmly to the doctrines of grace.

Divine sovereignty was the underlying framework that held Tyndale's life and theology together. He determinedly believed in the absolute sovereignty of God in His reign over all things.[3] Reformed doctrine fueled Tyndale's implacable drive in life and ministry. At the heart of his theology was the belief that God's sovereignty extended

---

3   Daniell, *William Tyndale*, 150.

from the control and order of the created universe to the salvation of undeserving sinners. Brian Edwards writes:

> Tyndale . . . knew that the cause of the corrupt state of the Church was its corrupt doctrine, and until the doctrine of the Church was corrected, the abuses would continue. On this turned the whole issue of the Reformation. The evangelical reformers were forced out of the Church of Rome, not because they could not accept the corrupt practices, but because they early discovered that the corrupt doctrines could never be changed.[4]

Before we examine the daring mission of William Tyndale, we must investigate the core beliefs that fueled the heart of this man who was such a driving force for God. In particular, we will focus upon the five truths of radical corruption, sovereign election, definite atonement, irresistible call, and preserving grace. These glorious doctrines of grace gave Tyndale confidence to persevere through difficult and dangerous times that could not be removed even by the fire at the stake or the noose of the martyr.

Radical Corruption

Tyndale believed in the total depravity of the human race. In this, Tyndale stood shoulder to shoulder with the biblical authors and other Reformers. He affirmed that the original sin of Adam brought about the fall and ruin of the entire human race. Therefore, all people are born in sin, a state inherited from Adam. Thus, all men are unable to save themselves apart from divine grace. He writes, "The

---

4   Edwards, 70.

fall of Adam has made us heirs of the vengeance and wrath of God, and heirs of eternal damnation; and has brought us into captivity and bondage under the devil."[5] It was Tyndale's conviction that original sin subjected the entire human race to sin, death, and judgment.

Tyndale taught that at the moment of conception, all people inherit a radically sin-corrupted nature:

> By nature, through the fall of Adam, are we the children of wrath, heirs of the vengeance of God by birth, yea, and from our conception. And we have our fellowship with damned devils, under the power of darkness and rule of Satan, while we are yet in our mother's wombs; and though we do not show the fruits of sin [as soon as we are born,] yet we are full of the natural poison, whereof all sinful deeds spring, and cannot but sin outwards, (be we never so young,) [as soon as we are able to work,] if occasion be given: for our nature is to do sin, as is the nature of a serpent to sting.[6]

Tyndale strongly maintained that every part of human nature is corrupted by sin, and sin affects the entire person—mind, will, and affections. This inherited condition renders every person fatally polluted by deadly poison. Tyndale writes of the comprehensive effects of Adam's sin upon every person:

> With what poison, deadly, and venomous hate hates a man his enemy! With how great malice of mind, inwardly, do we slay and murder! With what violence and rage, yea, and with how fervent

---

5   Tyndale, "A Pathway into the Holy Scripture," in *Works,* 1:17.
6   Ibid., 1:14.

list commit we advoutry, fornication, and such like uncleaness!
With what pleasure and dedication, inwardly, serves a glutton his
belly! With what diligence deceive we! How busily we seek the
things of this world![7]

So great is this radical corruption, it renders every member of
the human race abominable and guilty before a holy God. Tyndale
wrote:

Whatsoever we do, think, or imagine, is abominable in the sight
of God. [For we can refer nothing unto the honor of God; neither
is His law, or will, written in our members or in our hearts: neither
is there any more power in us to follow the will of God, than in a
stone to ascend upward of his own self.][8]

Total depravity has so devastated the human race, Tyndale
believed, that it causes man to be born in a state of moral inability. In
other words, fallen man cannot see or feel his need for saving grace.
He wrote, "We are as it were asleep in so deep blindness, that we can
neither see nor feel what misery, thraldom, and wretchedness we are
in, till Moses come and wake us, and publish the law."[9] In this fallen
state, sinful man is unconscious of his desperate need for the gospel.
Only the law can awaken him to the ruin of his spiritual condition.

But even when the law reveals his need for salvation, he cannot
do what the law requires. Tyndale explains, "It is not possible for a

---

7   Ibid., 1:17.
8   Ibid., 1:17–18.
9   Ibid., 1:18.

natural man to consent to the law."[10] Here Tyndale affirmed that sinful man is so debilitated by the fall of Adam that he is entirely unable to do anything that pleases God.

Tyndale believed that human nature is inherently evil, producing wicked thoughts and deeds. He taught:

> Of nature we are evil, therefore we both think and do evil, and are under vengeance under the law, convict to eternal damnation by the law, and are contrary to the will of God in all our will.[11]

Fallen man, he affirmed, is bound by his depraved nature:

> Our nature cannot but sin, if occasions be given, except that God of His special grace keep us back.[12]

Consequently, sinful man cannot do anything acceptable to God:

> How is it possible to do anything well in the sight of God, while we are yet in captivity and bondage under the devil, and the devil possesses us altogether, and holds our hearts, so that we cannot once consent unto the will of God?[13]

According to Tyndale's understanding, sin imprisons every unbeliever, preventing him from any movement toward God. He

---

10 Ibid.
11 Ibid., 1:14.
12 William Tyndale, "Exposition of the First Epistle of St. John," in *Works,* 2:151.
13 Tyndale, *Works,* 1:497–98.

compared every newly born baby to a young serpent, full of deadly poison ready to be released. Tyndale wrote:

> As a serpent, yet young, or yet unbrought forth, is full of poison, and cannot afterward (when the time is come, and occasion given) but bring forth the fruits thereof; and as an adder, a toad, or a snake, is hated of man, not for the evil that it has done, but for the poison that is in it, and hurt which it cannot but do: so are we hated of God, for that natural poison, which is conceived and born with us, before we do any outward evil.[14]

Tyndale held that Satan controls all unconverted souls. Tyndale believed the power of Satan in the hearts of unbelievers causes them to be under his dominion:

> The law and will of the devil is written as well in our hearts as in our members, and we run headlong after the devil with full zeal, and the whole swing of all the power we have; as a stone cast up into the air comes down naturally of his own self, with all the violence and swing of his own weight.[15]

Man's will is in bondage to the prince of darkness. His volitional capacity is held captive to do the devil's will. Tyndale wrote:

> The devil is our lord, and our ruler, our head, our governor, our prince, yea, and our god. And our will is locked and knit faster

---

14 Ibid., 1:14.
15 Ibid., 1:17.

unto the will of the devil, than could a hundred thousand chains
bind a man unto a post.[16]

Tyndale rejected the false notion of the freedom of the human
will, affirming that man's will is imprisoned by the devil. Tyndale
asserted that every person is born spiritually dead. Therefore, every
unconverted individual is held by the dominion of the devil:

> The text is plain: we were stone dead, and without life or power to
> do or consent to good. The whole nature of us was captive under
> the devil, and led at his will. And we were as wicked as the devil
> now is . . . and we consented unto sin with soul and body, and
> hated the law of God.[17]

Tyndale maintained that the unconverted soul is possessed by
the depraved lusts of the devil himself:

> We be always sinners, though not of purpose and malice after the
> nature of damned devils, but of infirmity and frailty of our flesh.[18]

Those who think they are without sin, he insisted, are self-deceived.
The spiritually blind cannot see their need for God and His grace:

> If we think there is no sin in us, we are beguiled and blind, and the
> light of God's word is not in us.[19]

---

16 Ibid.
17 Ibid., 2:199.
18 Ibid., 2:152.
19 Ibid., 2:150.

In short, Tyndale affirmed that all mankind is deserving of eternal damnation:

> We are all sinners without exception. And the Scripture witnesses that we are damnable sinners, and that our nature is to sin: which corrupt and poisoned nature, though it be begun to be healed, yet it is never thorough whole until the hour of death.[20]

> We were sinners and enemies to God . . . our hearts were as dead unto all good working as the members of him whose soul is departed.[21]

This doctrine alone could account for the cruel treatment he faced in the world.

Tyndale stated that the entire human race is like a corpse without a soul and spiritually dead. John Piper concludes: "This view of human sinfulness set the stage for Tyndale's grasp of the glory of God's sovereign grace in the gospel."[22] This is the fatal condition in which all unregenerate humans exist.

Sovereign Election

Tyndale was committed to the biblical teaching of the sovereign election of God. He believed God acted before time began, in eternal love, in choosing a people whom He would save. God set His heart upon a people, elected out of the mass of fallen humanity, to be His own possession. This election of man was not based upon

---

20 Ibid.
21 Ibid., 2:199.
22 Piper, 39.

any foreseen choice within man. Rather, it was entirely by the free exercise of God's will:

> Predestination . . . and salvation are clean taken out of our hands, and put in the hands of God only . . . for we are so weak and so uncertain, that if it stood in us, there would of a truth be no man saved; the devil, no doubt, would deceive us.[23]

Tyndale was clear that God set His affections upon His elect in eternity past. He stated that God sovereignly chose to love them with a saving love. Tyndale also said that God chose to love His elect for His own glory and for their good:

> God is ever fatherly minded toward the elect members of His church. He loved them, before the world began, in Christ.[24]

> The end of all things shall be unto His glory and the profit of the elect.[25]

Tyndale understood it was God who first chose His elect, not sinners who first chose Him, and that God made this distinguishing choice in eternity past. This is to say, all saving grace is traced back to this sovereign choice of God unto salvation:

> God chose them [the elect] first, and they not God.[26]

---

23 Tyndale, *Works,* 1:505.
24 William Tyndale, *An Answer to Sir Thomas More's Dialogue* (1531; repr., Cambridge, England: The Parker Society, 1850), 111.
25 Tyndale, *Works*, 2:171.
26 Tyndale, *Answer*, 35.

In Christ God chose us, and elected us before the beginning of the world, created us anew by the word of the gospel, and put His Spirit in us, for because that we should do good works.[27]

Divine election is unto salvation, not to be explained away as merely to service. The divine choice determines those chosen would be no longer in Adam, but in Christ. Tyndale taught that election is unto eternal life:

By grace (that is to say, by favor) we are plucked out of Adam, the ground of all evil, and grafted in Christ, the root of all goodness.[28]

You are chosen for Christ's sake to the inheritance of eternal life.[29]

Tyndale explained that sovereign election leads to the personal knowledge of Christ in the gospel. The elect are chosen by God to know Christ:

In Christ God loved us, His elect and chosen, before the world began, and reserved us unto the knowledge of his Son and of His holy gospel.[30]

Tyndale believed not all who attend church are numbered among the elect. Only those chosen by God make up the true church. He explained:

---

27 Tyndale, *Works*, 1:77.
28 Ibid., 1:14.
29 Ibid., 1:49.
30 Ibid., 1:14.

There shall be in the church a fleshly seed of Abraham and a spiritual; a Cain and an Abel; an Ishmael and an Isaac; an Esau and a Jacob; as I have said, a worker and a believer; a great multitude of them that be called, and a small flock of them that be elect and chosen.[31]

While many contend that election is a dangerous doctrine to be feared and withheld from people, Tyndale held the complete opposite. He believed this divine truth emboldens the preacher because it ensures the ultimate success of his preaching ministry. No matter how hardened man's heart may be, Tyndale insisted, sovereign election guarantees the reception of the gospel:

When Christ is . . . preached . . . the hearts of them which are elect and chosen, begin to wax soft and melt at the bounteous mercy of God.[32]

In summary, Tyndale believed that sovereign election exalts God as worthy of all honor. This truth sets God apart from man and above him. God is not subject to man's wisdom or will. This truth of unconditional election exalts God as the supreme ruler over man:

Why does God open one man's eyes and not another's? Paul (Rom. 9) forbids to ask why; for it is too deep for man's capacity. God we see is honoured thereby, and His mercy set out and the more seen in the vessels of mercy. But the popish can suffer God to have no

---

31 Tyndale, *Answer*, 107.
32 Tyndale, *Works*, 1:19.

secret, hid to Himself. They have searched to come to the bottom of His bottomless wisdom: and because they cannot attain to that secret, and be too proud to let it alone, and to grant themselves ignorant, with the apostle, that knew no other than God's glory in the elect; they go and set up free-will with the heathen philosophers, and say that a man's free-will is the cause why God chooses one and not another, contrary unto all the Scripture.[33]

Tyndale affirmed that sovereign election glorifies God, humbles man, initiates salvation, and honors Scripture. This doctrine gave Tyndale great confidence in all his endeavors as he was reliant upon God for all things.

Particular Redemption

Tyndale believed in the vicarious atonement of Jesus Christ. While his statements regarding the extent of Christ's saving death are not as definitive as those of other Reformers—due in part to the fact that he was principally a Bible translator, not a commentator or practicing theologian—he affirmed the doctrine that the death of Christ was offered for the redemption of those chosen by God before the foundation of the world. He affirmed that Christ, on the cross, purchased salvation for all believers. He writes: "Christ's blood has purchased life for us, and has made us the heirs of God; so that heaven comes by Christ's blood. If you would obtain heaven with the merits and deservings of your own works, yea, and shame the blood of Christ; and unto you were Christ dead in vain."[34] Here, "us" refers to believers only.

---

33 Tyndale, *Answer*, 191.
34 Tyndale, *Works*, 1:65.

The finished work of Christ upon the cross, Tyndale held, made a real satisfaction for sin: "Christ's works only justify you, and make satisfaction for your sin, and not your own works."[35] The key word in this statement is "only," and it is reflected in the Reformation motto *solus Christus*—Christ alone. Rome said Christ saves, but something of man must always be added to what Christ did at the cross to achieve salvation. Tyndale insisted that the substitutionary death of Christ may not be supplemented with anything, lest we make His sacrifice of no effect. No human works can be added to His finished work. Tyndale wrote: "The promise of the mercy is made you for Christ's work's sake, and not for your own works' sake."[36] Salvation is to promote the glory of Christ, not man's acclaim.

Tyndale asserted that the cross of Christ did not merely make salvation possible, with man's response necessary to make it a saving atonement. Instead, he wrote that Christ actually *purchased* salvation for all who would believe, securing for them eternal life. He maintained: "I am heir of heaven by grace and Christ's purchasing."[37] If Christ purchased salvation for all, then all will be saved. But He died for the true church, and it is only believers who are saved. John Piper attributes to Tyndale the teaching of "blood-bought sovereign grace."[38]

Tyndale was emphatic that human works make no contribution toward man's salvation: "God has never promised that your own works shall save you, therefore faith in your own works can never quiet your conscience, or certify you before God."[39] Again, Tyndale

35 Ibid., 1:509.
36 Ibid.
37 Ibid., 1:22.
38 Piper, 42.
39 Tyndale, *Works*, 1:509.

wrote, "Heaven, justifying, forgiveness, all gifts of grace, and all that is promised them, they receive of Christ, and by His merits freely."[40]

There is nothing that man can do to earn eternal life. All salvation is by Christ alone. He said, "He is our Redeemer, Deliverer, Reconciler, Mediator, Intercessor, Advocate, Attorney, Solicitor, our Hope, Comfort, Shield, Protection, Defender, Strength, Health, Satisfaction and Salvation."[41] From beginning to end, Christ is everything in salvation and is worthy of praise and exaltation that none may boast in His glorious presence.

Irresistible Call

Tyndale held that divine election is inseparably linked to the irresistible call of the Spirit. He understood that God's choice of individual sinners leads to the work of the Spirit in the new birth. Those whom the Father has chosen will be brought by the Spirit to new life. They will hate their sin, see their need for grace, and believe in Christ:

> Of the whole multitude of the nature of man, whom God has chosen, and to whom He has appointed mercy and grace in Christ, to them sends He His Spirit; which opens their eyes, shows them their misery, and brings them unto the knowledge of themselves; so that they hate and abhor themselves.[42]

According to Tyndale, the new birth is a sovereign work of God. Regeneration, he believed, is a monergistic act of divine creation in

---

40 Tyndale, *Answer*, 109.
41 Tyndale, *Works*, 1:19.
42 Ibid., 1:89.

the spiritually dead soul, meaning that God does the work without
the cooperation of the individual:

> We are, in . . . our second birth, God's workmanship and creation
> in Christ; so that, as he which is yet unmade has no life or power
> to work, no more had we, till we were made again in Christ.[43]

Where no spiritual life exists because of man's sinful nature, God
must create new life. There must be a supernatural work that reverses
the heart's affections:

> The Spirit must first come, and wake him out of his sleep with
> the thunder of the law, and fear Him, and show him his miserable
> estate and wretchedness; and make him abhor and hate himself,
> and to desire help; and then comfort him again with the pleasant
> rain of the gospel.[44]

In this sovereign work of the Spirit, Tyndale believed that saving
faith comes exclusively from God. Man can only believe when God
enables him to trust in Christ:

> Faith springs not of man's fantasy, neither is it in any man's power
> to obtain it; but it is altogether the pure gift of God poured into
> us freely, without all manner of doing of us, without deserving and
> merits, yea, and without seeking for us; and is . . . God's gift and
> grace, purchased through Christ."[45]

---

43 Ibid., 2:200.
44 Ibid., 1:498.
45 Ibid., 1:53.

Concerning the grace to believe, Tyndale affirmed that not only is eternal life the free gift of God but so also is the gift to believe. Thus, salvation is all of grace. Tyndale wrote:

> True faith is . . . the gift of God; and is given to sinners, after the law has passed upon them, and has brought their consciences unto the brim of desperation and sorrows of hell.[46]

Consequently, Tyndale resisted the false notion that man has free will to believe in Christ; this he saw as an impossibility because of the spiritual death in man. He wrote:

> Beware of the leaven that says, we have power in our free-will, before the preaching of the gospel, to deserve grace, to keep the law of congruity, or God to be unrighteous. . . . And when they say our deeds with grace deserve heaven, say thou with Paul, (Romans 6) that "everlasting life is the gift of God through Jesus Christ our Lord."[47]

The Spirit grants saving faith to elect sinners, enabling them to believe. True conversion occurs when the Spirit awakens the slumbering sinner out of his death and gives him faith to believe upon Christ. Tyndale taught:

> Scripture ascribes both faith and works, not unto us, but to God only, to whom they belong only, and to whom they are appropriate, whose gifts they are, and the proper work of His Spirit.[48]

---

46 Ibid., 1:12–13.
47 Ibid., 1:466.
48 Ibid., 1:56.

Tyndale understood that God must grant the divine gift of saving faith before the sinner can believe. The sinner is entirely dependent upon God for the capacity to believe. As a child cannot cause his own physical birth, so a sinner cannot cause his own birth from above. Regeneration is a sovereign act of God in which He raises the spiritually dead to believe:

> The will has no operation at all in the working of faith in my soul, no more than the child has in the begetting of his father: for Paul said, "It is the gift of God," and not of us.[49]

Tyndale recognized that God is the sole initiator of regeneration. The Spirit must first enlighten and give faith before any sinner can believe:

> Note now the order: first God give me light to see the goodness and righteousness of the law, and my own sin and unrighteousness; out of which knowledge springs repentance. ... Then the same Spirit works in my heart trust and confidence, to believe the mercy of God and His truth, that He will do as He has promised; which belief saves me.[50]

Tyndale affirmed that the Holy Spirit must create saving faith in the heart of the sinner if he is to believe the gospel. When the Word is preached, Tyndale taught, God bestows saving faith in the hearts of those who will believe. In other words, saving faith is bestowed by

---

49 Tyndale, *Answer*, 140.
50 Ibid., 195–96.

God through the preaching of the Word, it enters the unbelieving heart, and simultaneously the Word is believed. In that moment, the sinner is set free from his bondage to sin:

> When His word is preached, faith roots herself in the hearts of the elect; and as faith enters, and the word of God is believed, the power of God looses the heart from captivity and bondage under sin.[51]

A firm trust in Christ will not occur until God brings a man to the end of himself in order to fully trust in Him. There must be death to self if there is to be the birth of faith in Christ:

> It is not possible that Christ should come to a man, as long as he trusts in himself . . . or has any righteousness of his own, or riches of holy works.[52]

This is the point of division between Catholic and Protestant theology. Tyndale maintained that Roman Catholics say "a man's free will is the cause why God chooses one and not another, contrary to all Scripture. Paul said that it comes not from the will, nor of deed, but of the mercy of God."[53] Tyndale clearly shows the chasm between Catholics and Protestants. The former believe the free will of man supersedes God's choice, while the later affirm the complete and total sovereign will of God.

To say that fallen man has the ability in himself to believe, Tyndale stated, is to rob God of His glory. He wrote, "Is it not a forward

---

51 Tyndale, *Works,* 1:54.
52 Ibid., 1:22.
53 Tyndale, *Answer,* 191–92.

and perverse blindness, to teach how a man can do nothing of his own self; and yet presumptuously take upon them the greatest and highest work of God, even to make faith in themselves of their own power, and of their own false imagination and thoughts?"[54]

From before the foundation of the world, God chose all who would be in Christ, and He calls those individuals to Himself by granting the gift of grace and faith to believe in Him. This glorious truth demands the praise and worship of Christ, who alone is worthy of all honor in the saving of His people.

Preserving Grace

Tyndale affirmed the perseverance of the saints, the doctrine that those chosen in Christ cannot be taken from the Father's hand nor fall away again into condemnation. Simply stated, all who truly repent and believe in Christ will never fall from grace. Tyndale maintained, "God's elect cannot so fall that they rise not again, because that the mercy of God ever waits upon them, to deliver them from evil, as the care of a kind father waits upon his son to warn him and to keep him from occasions, and to call him back again if he be gone too far."[55] Despite the difficulty Tyndale constantly faced in this life, he held firmly to the glorious truth that all believers who stumble and fall will be upheld by the sustaining grace of God.

With the final outcome guaranteed, Tyndale taught that all believers are eternally secure in Christ: "Life eternal and all good things are promised unto faith and belief; so that he that believes on Christ shall be safe."[56] All who put their trust in Christ are forever

---

54 Tyndale, *Works,* 1:56.
55 Tyndale, *Answer,* 36.
56 Tyndale, *Works,* 1:65.

safe from divine condemnation and are delivered from the eternal wrath to come.

Tyndale asserted that all believers may enjoy the assurance of their salvation. He believed that a converted sinner "feels so great mercy, love, and kindness in God, that he is sure in himself how that it is not possible that God should forsake him, or withdraw His mercy and love from him; and boldly cry out with Paul, saying, 'Who shall separate us from the love that God loved us withal?'"[57] Tyndale was convinced by the testimony of Scripture that God will never forsake or withdraw His love from one who believes in Christ.

A Place to Stand

As Tyndale served God, he did so with a high view of God. He strongly believed that there are no external constraints upon God. The Almighty Lord is free to do as He sovereignly chooses. No one can force Him to act in a manner contrary to His divine prerogative. Tyndale wrote: "God is free, and [is] no further bound than He binds Himself."[58] The only restraints upon God, he maintained, are the restraints He places upon Himself within His own holy character and perfect will.

Regardless of the opposition he faced, Tyndale was confident that God freely acts in history and ordains all events according to His perfect counsel. Even the greatest of men, including kings and governors, are subject to His supreme will: "God [has] all tyrants in His hand, and lets them not do whatsoever they would, but as much only as He appoints them to do."[59]

---

57 Ibid., 1:22.
58 Ibid., 1:316.
59 Ibid., 1:140.

In other words, God sovereignly raises up one ruler and lowers another. These divinely appointed leaders do only as God appoints them to do. This included the king of England, Henry VIII, who opposed Tyndale's translation efforts. Tyndale wrote:

> God makes the king head over His realm; even so gives He him commandment to execute the laws upon all men indifferently. For the law is God's, and not the king's. The king is but a servant, to execute the law of God . . . God hath made governors in the world . . . they have received their offices of God, to minister and to do service.[60]

Tyndale viewed his entire life as being in subjection to the great purposes of God, even in his hours of greatest adversity. As he carried out his daring mission, these truths emboldened Tyndale to take great risks with his life in order to fulfill what he believed was God's will. He acknowledged that his work would only advance "if it be God's will that I shall further labour in His harvest."[61] Regardless of what rose up against him, Tyndale was convinced that the eternal purposes of God were moving forward according to His eternal, sovereign plan. With strong, passionate reliance upon God, Tyndale pressed on in his work with mounting confidence in the overruling providence of sovereign God. It would be these overarching doctrines that would fuel his faith and give him an unflinching confidence in God.

60 Ibid., 1:334.
61 Ibid., 1:397.

3

The Perilous Work Begins

*Translations of the Bible were among the most powerful
agencies for the promotion of the Reformation. Luther translated
the Bible into German; Calvin made a French translation.
The translation of the Bible into Dutch was a great help
to the Reformation in the Netherlands. Now Tyndale set
to work to translate the Bible into English.*[1]

—B.K. KUIPER

If William Tyndale was anything, he was audacious—a man
emboldened to take great risks in fulfilling his dangerous mission
for God. Never one to sit back passively, nor one to cower at the
prospect of a tumultuous journey, Tyndale was ever advancing in the
face of mounting opposition while pursuing his goal of providing his
countrymen with an English Bible. No greater gift could be given
to any people than to present them with the Scriptures in their own

---

1   B.K. Kuiper, *The Church in History* (Grand Rapids, Mich.: Eerdmans,
      1951), 277.

language. Arguably, Tyndale made the single greatest contribution to this history-altering movement that was the English Reformation. However, the gift he provided to the English-speaking world did not come cheap. It came at a great cost for Tyndale, as he gave up a life of comfort and, ultimately, his very life.

The translation of the English Bible by Tyndale was a demanding work that did not occur all at once. It came in successive stages over an entire decade. In 1525, Tyndale first translated the New Testament in Cologne, though its printing was unexpectedly halted. In 1526, he revised this translation and successfully printed it in Worms. Four years later, in 1530, Tyndale translated and printed the five books of Moses in Antwerp. The following year, in May 1531, Tyndale translated and printed the book of Jonah. Three years after that, Tyndale revised and reprinted his translation of Genesis and the New Testament in Antwerp. In 1535, another improved edition of the New Testament followed in Antwerp. The same year, 1535, Tyndale translated Joshua through 2 Chronicles, which was published posthumously by John Rogers in the Matthew Bible in 1537.

Having surveyed William Tyndale's unwavering commitment to the sovereign grace of God in salvation, we now proceed to a more careful examination of his efforts to translate the Bible for the English-speaking world.

As we begin to trace the daring mission of Tyndale, we will do so by moving chronologically through the various stages of his translation work. This chapter will focus upon Tyndale's first edition of the English New Testament, translated from the original Greek language and its attempted printing. This inaugural effort in 1525 laid a firm foundation upon which Tyndale would build subsequent revisions. A long journey began with this initial step, the first on the road to providing the English people with a sound translation of the Bible from the original Greek language.

Arrival in Germany

When he arrived in Europe in 1524, Tyndale traveled undercover as a soon-to-be fugitive from the English crown. His initial movement around the Continent is veiled in ambiguity. Some scholars think he traveled first to the German city of Hamburg, where a widow, Margaret Van Emerson, hosted him until he continued to Cologne. A noted Tyndale biographer, J.F. Mozley, argues that he first went to Wittenberg, Germany, where the famed Reformers Martin Luther and Philip Melanchthon were teaching at the University of Wittenberg. Mozley examined the registers of this institution and found a particular name under the date of May 27, 1524—Guillelmus Daltici ex Anglia. Mozley speculates that the name is a Latinized anagram for "William Tyndale from England,"[2] which Tyndale used to disguise his identity in order to preserve his anonymity.

If this entry was really made by Tyndale, then it is likely he interacted with Luther and Melanchthon concerning the work of God in Europe. Doubtless, they would have conversed about the translation of Scriptures into the languages of their respective peoples. A mere year or two earlier, in 1522, Luther had completed his translation of the New Testament into the German tongue. Tyndale's time in Wittenberg would also help account for his newly acquired knowledge of Hebrew, for he did not know the Old Testament language before leaving England.

---

2   J.F. Mozley, *William Tyndale* (1937; repr., Westport, Conn.: Greenwood, 1971), 53.

Tyndale would have remained in Wittenberg for nine or ten months, until about April 1525. During this time, he may have worked on his English translation of the New Testament. From there, Tyndale would have returned to Hamburg to send for his money from England in preparation for printing his new work.

With financial resources in hand, the time had arrived for Tyndale to print his English New Testament. In considering his options, he chose the German city of Cologne for the printing operation. The city employed many printers capable of producing and binding large runs of Tyndale's English translation. But in many ways, Cologne was an unlikely choice as a place to print an English translation of the New Testament. Only four years earlier, on April 18, 1521, Luther had stood trial a mere one hundred miles away in Worms, where he had been condemned as a heretic by Rome. When Tyndale arrived, Cologne was a Catholic bastion under the heavy-handed leadership of the Catholic archbishop-elector.

Cologne represented all that Tyndale had rejected in England. This pro-Catholic city reeked of the empty religious superstitions of Rome. Pilgrims flocked to its relics and idolatrous shrines; indulgences were offered for sale by unconverted priests. Towering over the city was the Cologne Cathedral, one of the largest structures on earth. Construction had begun three centuries earlier, and it remained unfinished in Tyndale's day. It was not until the nineteenth century, after centuries of inaction, that this ambitious building project would be completed. The cathedral allegedly housed the bones of the Magi who visited Christ at His birth. The skeletal remains proudly were showcased in the largest gold sarcophagus in Europe. This was Cologne—Romish, popish, religious, superstitious, and lost.

In resistance to the Reformation, the authorities issued a mandate to punish all authors of "Reformed heresy" in Cologne, as well as their printers. Rome established a local board of priests and theologians to censor all works that did not conform to Catholic doctrine. The translation and printing of any book without the authorization of the Catholic Church was strictly forbidden. A short time earlier, the books and pamphlets of Luther had been burned publicly before the front steps of this cathedral.

It was into this hostile environment that Tyndale stepped in order to print his translation of the English New Testament. He chose Cologne because it was a prosperous trading center. It possessed the largest market square of any city in Germany. Because it was a gathering place for international businessmen, the presence of another Englishman like Tyndale was not likely to arouse suspicion. The steady flow of business activity here made it easy for Tyndale to transfer the necessary funds from London to finance his print run.

Cologne was also positioned on the Rhine River, which provided access to the North Sea and thus to English ports. This made the shipment of the Bibles much easier than if it had to be carried out by land. An overland route would have entailed crude wagons and muddy roads and would have subjected shipments to unexpected government inspections, increasing the danger of arrest and possible death. Shipping the Bibles by water was a vastly superior means of transportation.

Moreover, Cologne offered a wide selection of printers from whom Tyndale could choose for his project. There was also a wide array of booksellers in Cologne who kept the city's printers in profitable business. Though Cologne was a Catholic city, some local printers were willing to risk arrest in order to print Reformed works for financial gain. It was difficult for the Catholic authorities to monitor every printing endeavor. In order to remain undercover, many printers would print controversial works without a title page, thus omitting their names. For these reasons, Cologne was ideally suited for this ambitious work. Here, Tyndale would launch his audacious project on the very doorsteps of hell.

The First Printing

Tyndale approached Peter Quentell to fulfill the task of printing his New Testament. Quentell was a second-generation printer who had learned his trade from his father, an eminent printer. Tyndale began this project by giving Quentell the gospel of Matthew in English. He may have also given him the gospel of Mark as the next book in line. The intended print run was between three thousand and six thousand copies, though the men probably agreed on three thousand.

The printing of the New Testament by Quentell was elaborate for the day. The gospel of Matthew begins dramatically with a full-page woodcut portrait of the Apostle. Matthew is shown with pen in hand, dipping his writing instrument into an ink bottle held by an angel. At every chapter division, there are large illuminations. The inside margins are filled with biblical cross-references, taking the interested reader to supportive passages. The outside margins are sprinkled with expository explanations of the biblical text. Asterisks in the study notes identify for the reader the specific passage being explained. Tyndale's Bible bears a striking resemblance to Luther's September Testament, printed three years earlier. Tyndale's New Testament, however, was printed at a smaller size than Luther's version. It was intended to be compact enough to be carried unnoticed. After all, it was unlawful to own a copy of this work.

Both the translation and printing were done under the shroud of absolute secrecy. Tyndale knew all too well the severe consequences that would befall him if he were caught carrying out his mission. Consequently, this first version of Tyndale's Bible was printed without a title page. This would allow Tyndale's identity to remain unknown and would help protect his safety. Moreover, the publisher's name and city were absent, protecting Quentell in this risky project.

As the initial sheet was pulled off the press in Quentell's print shop, still wet with ink, the printed Word of God was being made available to the common man in the English language for the first time. No longer would the Scripture be hidden in the guise of another language.

Tyndale could not carry out this heroic task alone. At his side was a fellow Englishman, William Roye, who acted as his personal assistant. Roye, like Tyndale, was a Cambridge man with Reformed ideals. He was a Franciscan friar from Greenwich who had become a renegade from the Catholic Church and fled for safety to the European Continent. He studied under Luther at the University of Wittenberg, graduating in June 1525. If Tyndale did indeed travel to Wittenberg, he would have made connection with Roye there.

In his writings, Tyndale explained that he had been waiting for another individual to join him in Europe. This unnamed person would probably have been coming from England. If so, it has been surmised that this person was Miles Coverdale, the later compiler of the Coverdale Bible. While Tyndale was waiting for this other person, Roye approached him and offered his help.[3] Tyndale accepted

---

3   William Tyndale, "Preface to the Reader: The Parable of the Wicked Mammon," in *Works,* 1:38.

his offer, and the two began this dangerous task together. It would be Roye's duty to help prepare Tyndale's translation for the press.

The partnership between Tyndale and Roye was awkward, however, and often strained. Tyndale described Roye as a "crafty" individual, which made it difficult for him to trust him. Given the covert nature of their work, this lingering suspicion was a detriment for Tyndale. Roye, Tyndale stated, had a tongue that was "able not only to make fools stark mad, but also to deceive the wisest."[4] Though they would eventually part company, Roye worked alongside Tyndale during the printing of the first edition of the New Testament in Cologne.

Sources for the Translation

The primary source for Tyndale's translation of the New Testament was the newly compiled Greek text produced by the humanist scholar Desiderius Erasmus of Rotterdam. Tyndale worked from Erasmus' third edition, compiled less than ten years earlier. His work in the original language distinguished his translation from what the Oxford professor John Wycliffe had accomplished one hundred and forty years earlier. Because he worked exclusively from the Latin Vulgate, Wycliffe's work was limited in its accuracy. Tyndale's New Testament was the first English translation from the Greek text.

The New Testament had been written in *koinē* Greek, the common language of the first century. This form of Greek was the most widely used language in the eastern Mediterranean region. The early Christians also used a Greek version of the Old Testament called the Septuagint. Around the beginning of the fifth century, the scholar

---

4   Ibid., 1:39.

Jerome (c. 347–420) translated the Greek and Hebrew into the lingua franca of his day, Latin. This text became known as the Vulgate, from the Latin word *vulgar*, referring to the common language of the people. Over time, the Catholic Church adopted the Vulgate as its official text of Scripture, with authority superseding the Greek and Hebrew or any vernacular translations. The Vulgate spread across the Roman Empire, including the British Isles, over the next thousand years.

The Vulgate was successful because Latin was the common language of the Roman Empire. However, Greek and Latin are fundamentally different languages. Latin cannot convey the precise meaning of the original Greek language. Consequently, the Vulgate translation of the New Testament fell short in bringing out the true meaning of the Greek text.

With the advent of the Renaissance, a new breed of European scholars was born. These thinkers expressed their displeasure with the vagueness of the Vulgate. Among its other effects, the intellectual movement of the Renaissance gave rise to a renewed interest in the Greek language. When the Vulgate was examined against the original Greek, it was found to be wanting. And so, driven by a love for the original languages and fueled by the heady intellectual climate of his day, Erasmus traveled throughout Europe in order to compile the best ancient manuscripts of the Bible in the Latin and Greek languages.

Erasmus' New Testament was titled *Novum instrumentum*, which means "new instrument." This new text for the New Testament was to be his "new instrument'" to bring about reform in the education of the church. Published in 1516, it was the first new Latin translation of the New Testament in more than one thousand years. It proved popular, as from 1516 to 1522, 3,300 copies of the *Novum instrumentum* were sold. Erasmus set the Latin version side by side with his compiled Greek text. This parallel Bible was the first time the Greek text of Scripture was ever in print.

This Greek New Testament became the foundation for every new version of Scripture translated into a European language for many years to come. This Greek text is what Luther used in 1521–22 to translate the New Testament into German. It was said that Erasmus laid the egg, but Luther hatched it and gave it to his people. Likewise, Erasmus' Greek text was the basis of Tyndale's translation of the New Testament into English.

In addition to Erasmus' Greek, Tyndale had before him Luther's new German translation of the New Testament. After the Diet of Worms, Luther was kidnapped by his friends and taken to the Wartburg Castle. There, he translated the Bible from the original Greek into the German language. He did so under the protection of Frederick III, elector of Saxony, and he did it at an incredible pace, completing the project in only eleven weeks—from December 1521 to February 1522. Melanchthon, a Greek scholar, and other linguistic specialists later edited Luther's work. Copies of his New Testament began to come off the press in September 1522. Some two thousand to five thousand copies were printed by December.

Luther's New Testament was tremendously popular in Protestant areas throughout Germany. This widespread acceptance resulted in the development of a standardized written form of the German language. By 1534, Luther and others translated the Old Testament and had it printed. Eighty-seven editions of Luther's New Testament were published in the dialect of High German and some nineteen editions were printed in the dialect of Low German. In a relatively short time, more than two hundred thousand copies had been sold, a staggering distribution.

Tyndale, who was proficient in German, consulted the second and third editions of Luther's September Testament, as the 1522 edition was called. As he translated into English, Tyndale used much that he found to be helpful in Luther's German Bible. While following the Greek text as his primary source, Tyndale found Luther's German to be a helpful secondary source. Nevertheless, Tyndale proved to be his own man in doing his translation work, often differing from Luther in his choice of words and phrases.

As previously mentioned, Tyndale also relied upon Erasmus' improved Latin version. This new version of the Latin text contained about four hundred alterations to the text of the Vulgate. Erasmus had toured the monasteries of Europe and compiled the best available manuscripts in his work in improving upon Jerome's Vulgate. With this modern Latin version, which appeared with Erasmus' Greek version, Tyndale had another reference with which to make a comparison. The new Latin version was completed in 1516, the year before the Reformation began.

B.F. Westcott, who later edited an influential critical text of the Greek New Testament, noted Tyndale's dependence upon Erasmus' Latin version of the New Testament: "There is, however, one other authority who had greater influence upon Tindale than the Vulgate or Luther. The Greek text of the New Testament published by Erasmus, which Tindale necessarily used, was accompanied by an original Latin version in which Erasmus faithfully rendered the text he had printed. This translation is very frequently followed by Tindale."[5]

---

5   Brooke Foss Westcott, *A General View of the History of the English Bible* (New York: Macmillan, 1916), 135.

As Tyndale carried out his translation work, there is no indication that he consulted John Wycliffe's New Testament. This primitive English version had been translated nearly a century and a half earlier by the Oxford professor who launched the Lollard movement in fourteenth-century England. Tyndale may not have wanted the influence of Wycliffe's choice of English words. Instead, he wanted to choose the best English words to convey the original language. Because he did not have access to another English translation, Tyndale's work was entirely original.

Features of the First Edition

The first sheets of Tyndale's New Testament that rolled off the press at the end of August 1525 were his prologue. Tyndale begins by issuing a welcome to the reader and then defends the need for an English translation. He explains what the two testaments are and shows the relationship between law and gospel. Tyndale also gives a summary of Luther's theology, especially focusing upon justification by faith alone. He then proceeds to an extended treatment of man's depravity and the nature of sin. Here, Tyndale enlarges upon Luther's prologue from his German translation. Tyndale often uses Luther's words, but subtracts from some of the German Reformer's thoughts in order to enlarge other truths.

In the prologue, Tyndale uses Luther's writings and theology to inform his own thinking. He takes Luther's thoughts and expands them with the use of his own words. Tyndale gives an introduction to several important doctrines, most especially justification by faith. He sets in stark contrast the law and gospel. He starts with the law, showing the need for the gospel, and proceeds directly to address the grace of God in the gospel. Though Tyndale uses his own words, the writings of Luther are a constant guide. Tyndale then expounds the gospel of Jesus Christ with great clarity.

This prologue to Tyndale's New Testament is his first confirmed writing of which we still have an original copy. He writes with constant reference to the Bible, using scriptural language and many biblical allusions. He writes as one deeply immersed in the Bible. Tyndale was not simply translating the Scriptures, but was personally absorbing them. In the prologue, Tyndale states:

> I have here translated (brethren and sisters most dear and tenderly beloved in Christ) the New Testament for your spiritual edifying, consolation, and solace: Exhorting instantly and beseeching those that are better seen in the tongues than I, and that have higher gifts of grace to interpret the sense of the Scripture and meaning of the Spirit, than I, to consider and ponder my labour, and that with the spirit of meekness. And if they perceive in any places that I have not attained the very sense of the tongue, or meaning of the Scripture, or have not given the right English word, that they put to their hands to amend it, remembering that so is their duty to do. For we have not received the gifts of God for ourselves only, or for to hide them, but for to bestow them unto the honouring of God and Christ, and edifying of the congregation, which is the body of Christ.[6]

In listing the books of the New Testament, Tyndale departs from Luther's two-tier approach. In his German Bible, Luther elevated to the top tier the four Gospels and Acts, along with the epistles of

---

6   William Tyndale, "A Pathway into the Holy Scripture," in *Works,* 1:7.

Paul, Peter, and John. On the lower tier, he included Hebrews, James, Jude, and Revelation. Tyndale instead affirms the equal importance of each of the twenty-seven canonical books of the New Testament.

The preeminent Tyndale scholar David Daniell writes, "This prologue is one of Tyndale's most important documents. It is, as it were, his first manifesto. . . . This Prologue is almost entirely theological exposition of Scripture: the short opening passages that are not about the necessity of reading Scripture."[7] So important was this prologue that Tyndale later expanded it and had it printed separately under the title *A Pathway into the Holy Scripture.*

Tyndale writes in his prologue as he translates—with plain, easy-to-understand vocabulary. His ideas are not abstract and vague, but concrete and structured. He is organized in thought and easy to follow. With commanding language and syntax, he refuses to use complex words and avoids the stiffness of technical terms. The genius of Tyndale lay in his ability to state profound truth in lucid ways. Daniell comments, "The aim is not to dazzle with verbal arabesque and flourishes, but to be clear to the humblest hearer."[8] The goal of bringing God's Word to the common people was ever before Tyndale.

As Tyndale translated the New Testament, he did so without an English dictionary to assist him with spellings and definitions. In fact, such a dictionary did not then exist. His assistant, Roye, was at his side, mostly to help with the physical and practical concerns of the project. However, Roye, who was well educated, would also have been available for linguistic consultation. Tyndale nevertheless stood virtually alone in this work, led only by the guiding hand of God.

---

7 Daniell, *William Tyndale*, 124.
8 Ibid., 126.

Brian Moynahan describes Tyndale's translation process in this way:

> Tyndale's primary source was Erasmus's Greek New Testament, already in its third edition by 1524, together with the Latin translation and notes, which accompanied the Greek text. He also had the Latin Vulgate, and Luther's 1521 September Testament. He had no Lollard Bible with him. He said that he had no man to "counterfeit" or imitate; "neither," he added, "was help with English of any that had interpreted the same or such like thing in the scripture beforetime."[9]

As Tyndale translated the Greek text into English, he did so with extraordinary ability and skill. His unique gift was translating in a manner that is personal and direct. He used the everyday words of the marketplace in order to have his work understood by the common man. Moreover, he arranged his well-chosen words in simple sentences to facilitate comprehension. He did not write for the elite in the academy, but for the man on the street. Tyndale wrote with the aim of bringing the truth of Scripture to the masses of common people. His style was contemporary, yet majestic. His work set the standard for all English translations that would follow.

Not only did Tyndale translate the words of Scripture but he also provided explanatory notes in the outside margins of many pages of his New Testament. For example, in the first twenty-two chapters of the gospel of Matthew, there are ninety marginal notes. These comments provide helpful interpretation to assist the reader in understanding the

---

9   Moynahan, 56.

biblical text. The English Reformer's goal was to instruct; he aimed to help the reader grasp the authorial intent of the passage.

Tyndale's notes are terse, especially when compared to Luther's longer study notes. As he did with the German Reformer's translation, Tyndale used Luther's notes as an aid—two-thirds of the ninety comments in Matthew 1–22 in Tyndale's translation are from Luther—but often shortened or modified them. Tyndale's tone also has a different emphasis than Luther's, being less polemical. As the German Reformer explains Scripture, he is often combative. Luther sometimes seems to go out of his way to insert anti-papal and anti-priestly comments. Tyndale, on the other hand, writes in a more expository manner.

A Temporary Setback

As the presses were running, an unexpected interruption occurred. After the first ten sheets were printed, government officials broke into the print shop. A raid immediately halted the undercover operation. The city authorities had been alerted to the covert work and burst into the room to put it to a stop. Since printing the Bible in the English language was considered heretical, the work was abruptly halted. The printing had reached as far as Matthew 22:12 when it was suddenly shut down. All materials left in the print shop were seized and became the official property of the local government.

The last sheet to be completed was designated signature *H*. This meant it was the eighth sheet printed, *H* being the eighth letter of the English alphabet. Each individual sheet would be cut into eight separate pages. This means a total of eighty pages of the New Testament had been printed. Approximately half of what had been printed was Tyndale's prologue.

The city authorities intended to arrest Tyndale and Roye. Capture would have meant certain death for these two subversive Englishmen. But Tyndale and his assistant managed to escape before they could be apprehended. They were also able to gather up some of the pages that had been printed and flee with them. As they withdrew, they traveled up the Rhine River to Worms. There, Tyndale continued his secretive translation and printing work. Six months later, in 1526, a completed copy of his New Testament came off the press.

Today, only one set of these eight finished sheets of this 1525 Cologne New Testament remains. It contains all that Quentell had printed, beginning with the prologue and including Matthew 1:1–22:12. The loose sheets were bound together into book form in the nineteenth century and reside in the British Library. This Cologne edition of Tyndale's New Testament was the first time any portion of the New Testament was translated from the original Greek and printed in English. Though only a relatively few pages were printed, these cut-down sheets were distributed in England and helped spread the cause of the Reformation. Eventually, these truths would extend to the world, influencing generations to come.

Many of you reading these pages know something of challenges faced in the pursuit of God's will. Some of you may be wandering about, as in a thick fog, uncertain about whether you can even move forward in accomplishing God's will. Still others of you are beginning a task that you believe is given to you by the Lord, but are already willing to abandon its cause because it has been initially unsuccessful or has met with great opposition. You are beginning to doubt whether this is God's mission for you because of this lack of success and the opposition you face. Could this be where you find yourself?

May it be that we learn from the life and fortitude of William Tyndale. Even as the print shop was raided and his work was abruptly halted, he persevered and continued working to the very end. This Englishman did not sound the retreat, nor did he take even one step back from his intended goal of bringing God's Word to the common people. May each of us likewise press on in service to the Lord and what His Word would have us do, always advancing with our eyes fixed ahead, never looking back. Let us not question the sovereign hand of God. Rather, let us set our gaze upon God and pursue, wherever He has placed us, the work for which He has gifted us. By His grace and for His glory, may we faithfully carry it out to its accomplished end.

4

New Testament
for a Plowboy

In all the towns and villages of Tyndale's country the holy pages
were opened, and the delighted readers found therein those treasures
of peace and joy which the martyr had known. Many cried out with
him, "We know that this Word is from God, as we know that fire
burns; not because anyone has told us, but because a Divine fire
consumes our hearts."... Tyndale had desired to set the world on
fire by his Master's Word, and that fire was kindled. [1]

—J.H. MERLE D'AUBIGNÉ

William Tyndale was a driven and determined man, an indomitable figure who could not be diverted from providing an
English Bible for his native land. The initial efforts by Tyndale to
have his New Testament printed in Cologne in 1525 were unexpectedly halted by a raid on the print shop. A lesser man might have quit,
concluding that his task must not be God's will. But not Tyndale.
The thought of abandoning his God-given mission was completely

---

1   D'Aubigné, *The Reformation in England*, 2:350.

foreign to this resilient Reformer. The sense of duty to God could not be quenched. Throwing caution to the wind, Tyndale fled swiftly south from Cologne to Worms to avoid arrest by officials who sought to shut down his unlawful enterprise. Come what may, Tyndale was driven to translate the New Testament into English. His goal remained unaltered: to allow a plowboy to know as much of Scripture as the pope.

Igniting this fiery passion within Tyndale's soul was his core belief that saving faith requires knowledge of the truth, which requires that one has the Word of God in his own language. No one can enter the kingdom of God, he maintained, apart from knowing the gospel truth. If the English people were to possess the saving knowledge of Jesus Christ, the tenacious Tyndale knew that having the Scriptures in English was crucial. What is more, he believed no Christian can be sanctified apart from the Word, making an English translation even more important. Tyndale wanted to make the Scriptures open and accessible to the English people, and he wanted to put the Bible in their hands, for their own eyes to read.

Compounding his sense of urgency, Tyndale had earlier witnessed that the leaders of the Roman Catholic Church did not know even the most basic truths pertaining to salvation. The priests themselves were horribly ignorant of the Scripture—the blind leading the blind. As a result, England was suffocating in spiritual fog. There was a stifling famine in the land for the Word of the Lord.

The mission before Tyndale was clear. He was heavily burdened for the eternal destiny of the English-speaking world. An English Bible was not optional, but mandatory. Without the Bible in English, Tyndale asserted, the preacher might as well be speaking to pigs:

It is truly as good to preach it to swine as to men, if you preach it in a tongue they understand not. How shall I prepare myself to God's commandments? How shall I be thankful to Christ for His kindness? How shall I believe the truth and promises which God has sworn, while you tell them unto me in a tongue which I understand not?[2]

When the language of the Bible cannot be understood, Tyndale recognized, there is no differentiation between swine and sinner. Simply put, if the message of the Scriptures cannot be comprehended, no one can enter the kingdom of God.

This chapter will focus on Tyndale's travel from Cologne to Worms, where he would see the English New Testament at last printed and shipped to his homeland. There are many unique aspects to examine in order to understand how Tyndale accomplished this incredible task. But one fact is unmistakable: Tyndale was persistent in carrying out this daring mission.

A New Base

In selecting the next city in which to print his New Testament, there were several criteria Tyndale knew must be met. First, his new base had to be a thriving city where he could conduct his work under the cover of the distractions of a heavily populated place. Second, the city had to have several print shops from which to choose. These printers had to have available to them the relatively new moveable type of the Gutenberg press so that they could print rapidly at a low cost. Third, the city had to be strategically located near a paper mill

2   Tyndale, *Works,* 1:234.

that could supply a large amount of quality paper. It would be far too expensive and slow to print on vellum. Fourth, the city had to be well positioned on a navigable river that flowed to the sea so that the Bibles could be distributed in an efficient manner. Considering all these factors, Tyndale decided upon Worms.

Long a staunchly loyal Catholic stronghold, Worms was where Luther was summoned to stand trial for heresy in April 1521. However, Rome's strategy backfired. It was here that Luther defied church tradition and ecclesiastical authority by saying, "My conscience is captive to the Word of God. I cannot and I will not recant anything, since it is neither safe nor right to go against conscience. I cannot do otherwise; here I stand, may God help me, Amen."[3]

Luther's bold stand for the Word catapulted him into the role of a champion of the people. The courage of this German giant fed a wellspring of Protestant belief in Worms. By 1525, the city had shifted its religious loyalties from Catholicism to Lutheran convictions. This meant that four years after Luther's trial, Worms was the best place for Tyndale to print his New Testament. In late 1525, Tyndale, accompanied by Roye, traveled down the Rhine River until he arrived at Worms.

Worms was perfectly situated on the Rhine River, providing the water route needed to export Tyndale's newly printed Bibles. This would allow his New Testaments to be loaded onto barges and floated north until they reached a North Sea port. The Bibles could then be transferred onto merchant ships sailing for England. The cost associated with transporting the Bibles from Worms to England was only

---

3 Martin Luther, *Luther's Works,* vol. 32, ed. George W. Forell (Philadelphia: Fortress, 1958), 113.

slightly greater than the cost to ship from Cologne. Ironically, these Bibles would float up the Rhine River past Cologne, where Tyndale's printing had been earlier aborted.

In addition, Worms provided Tyndale with the needed exposure to become more proficient in the Hebrew language. As he was preparing his English New Testament, he was also becoming skilled in translating the Old Testament. In the mid-sixteenth century, few scholars in England even knew Hebrew. Fewer still were able to teach it. But Worms was one of the rare places where it could be learned. A large Jewish community lived there, which would allow Tyndale to study and learn the ancient language of the Old Testament with learned Jewish men. The oldest Jewish house of worship in Europe, the *Hintere Judengasse* synagogue, was in Worms as well. This German city had a strong reputation for being "as good a place to study Hebrew as any in Christendom."[4] For these strategic reasons, Worms was Tyndale's second choice, after Cologne, to print his New Testament.

Upon his arrival in Worms, Tyndale immediately sought to find a suitable printer. His choice was Peter Schoeffer—son of the Mainz printing pioneer—who was regarded as the leading printer in the city. The business arrangement between Tyndale and Schoeffer was probably established early in 1526. Schoeffer's name does not appear on Tyndale's New Testament, undoubtedly to protect his anonymity as the printer. Nevertheless, various clues reveal that Tyndale's Bible was the work of Schoeffer. The Gothic type used in the printing, the distinctive watermarks on the paper, and the unique woodcuts for the illustrations all identify Schoeffer as its printer.

---

4   Moynahan, 77.

There were no standardized typefaces for printing in the six-teenth century. Each printer created his own letter forms. As Schoeffer attempted to complete the printing that had been started in Cologne, he was unable to match precisely the previous typeface's size and style. This discrepancy did not stop the project, though. Moynahan explains, "This was a book to be read in secret, not dis-played in a collection."[5] Schoeffer was eminently qualified to move this ambitious project forward and bring it to completion. Certainly, a different typeface would not halt this project.

To print Tyndale's New Testament, a high-quality paper was required. Printing on thinly shaved sheepskin or calfskin, known as vellum, would have been far too expensive for such a large print run. The paper requirement was met by a mill in Troyes, France. This plant, operated by the Le Bé family, produced high-quality paper, but at a higher price. Nevertheless, this important project, which would carry the gospel of Jesus Christ, was well worth this better product, and Schoeffer was able to obtain a large supply of quality paper from the Le Bé mills to fulfill Tyndale's order.

The paper from the Le Bé mills was manufactured using a technique invented in Italy two centuries earlier. It was made from cotton fibers rather than wood pulp, resulting in a strong and dura-ble paper. This innovation made a large print run possible and reasonable. To make the paper, a generous supply of flimsy white rags was needed. The rags were cut into thin strips, soaked in water, hung, and beaten dry. They were treated with soap to produce pulp, which, in turn, was dipped into warm water. A wooden frame with cross wires was lowered into the water. The frame was then lifted

---

5   Ibid.

out, and excessive water was removed from the sheets by pressing it between layers of felt. The sheets were hung and coated with a thin layer of wax and clay. They were dried and rubbed with flint. The result was paper, ready to be delivered in reams of twenty-five sheets to the print shops in Worms. Schoeffer was one of the main purchasers of this paper.

Features of the Worms Edition

Schoeffer printed Tyndale's New Testament in the smaller octavo format, meaning each sheet would be folded to produce sixteen pages of text on eight leaves. The Cologne version had been printed in the larger quarto format, with eight pages of text on four leaves. The Worms edition did not contain a prologue at the beginning. Illuminations were placed at the beginning of each New Testament book. There were also no chapter breaks as there were in the Cologne edition. Neither was there a title page in the Worms edition bearing Tyndale's name. In the preface to one of his subsequent works, *The Parable of the Wicked Mammon*, Tyndale explained that the omission of his identity was to protect his anonymity. All that mattered to Tyndale was the distribution of the English Bible into the hands of the common people. Tyndale cared nothing for personal accolades.

This smaller size of the Worms edition of the New Testament had several benefits. First, this version was more cost efficient. It required less paper and ink to print this format than the larger Cologne edition. Second, a smaller Bible would be easier to export to England because it would require less space on board a ship. Third, a smaller Bible would be easier to hide in cotton bales in order to smuggle it into England. Fourth, a smaller New Testament would be easier for the owner to carry in a coat pocket or bag without being noticed. In a day when the printed English New Testament was still illegal, smaller size was a definite asset.

As Tyndale translated Greek into English, he had a specific approach in mind. His preeminent objective was to make the English translation accurate to the biblical text and accessible to the average reader. Above all, the style must be energetic and captivate the reader. Tyndale scholar David Daniell praises the translation work of Tyndale in this Worms edition:

> The 1526 New Testament . . . is triumphantly the work of a Greek scholar who knew that language well, of a skilled translator who could draw on the Latin of the Vulgate and Erasmus, and German, for help when needed, but above all of a writer of English who was determined to be clear, however hard the work of being clear might be.[6]

Regarding Tyndale's translation work, several things should be noted. First, Tyndale sought a translation to be easily understood by the common person. He translated for the plowboy in the field, not the professor in the classroom. Daniell explains, "Tyndale goes for clear, everyday, spoken English"[7] that "makes the best sense for his ordinary English readers."[8] Tyndale's real genius lay in discovering the simplest English form to convey the profoundest Greek expressions. This accessible style of English was drawn from "the current language of the day."[9] In other words, Tyndale wrote in everyday

---

6 Daniell, *William Tyndale*, 141.
7 Ibid., 135.
8 Ibid., 136.
9 Ibid., 135.

language for the average person. Herein lies the broad appeal of his translation work.

Second, Tyndale intended for the reader to move at a brisk pace as he read the biblical text. As best he could, Tyndale chose simpler, one-syllable words over more complex, multiple-syllable words. The shorter the word, he believed, the easier it would be for the reader's eye to move across the page. He was convinced that shorter words often have more clarity than longer words. When more cumbersome words were necessary, Tyndale intentionally placed them toward the end of sentences so the verse would start with greater ease of reading. When possible, Tyndale turned Greek participial phrases into English clauses in order to place less demand on the reader. He also purposely gave attention to the rhythm of the sentence. Tyndale did all this to enhance an energetic cadence for the reader.

Third, Tyndale aimed to do more than to reach the mind. His intent was also to move the soul. Tyndale was as interested in the style of his language as he was in the substance of each word and phrase. He carefully crafted each aspect of his sentences so that the Holy Spirit would impart the truth in heart-moving fashion. Tyndale's mission was to create a work that not only teaches the mind but also "speaks to the heart."[10] In this, he was eminently successful.

This threefold approach was on Tyndale's mind as he weighed each word, phrase, clause, and sentence. In reality, he functioned as a mediator between the original Greek text and the English page. His purpose was to construct a translation that was accurate to the author's intent, flowed before the reader's eyes, and touched the

10 Ibid.

reader's heart. Through his laborious efforts, Tyndale was altering the course of English history.

In this Worms edition, Tyndale chose not to include the opening prologue he had earlier included in the Cologne edition. He also did not add the marginal notes from his 1525 version. Instead, he wrote a short postscript at the end of his New Testament. This concluding word was intended to call the reader to action in response to the truth of Scripture.

In a straightforward appeal, this final postscript is expressed with swelling passion. Tyndale summons the reader to carefully consider the priceless treasure in their hands—the written Word of God. Moreover, he calls them to respond to its message in repentance and faith in Jesus Christ.

In this postscript, Tyndale holds out the spiritual riches of the gospel to morally bankrupt sinners. He calls the reader to entrust himself to God through faith in Christ, and not to trust in his own merit. Tyndale writes:

"Give diligence, Reader, I exhort you, that you come with a pure mind, and as the Scripture says with a single eye, unto the words of health and of eternal life, by the which, if we repent and believe them, we are born anew, created afresh, and enjoy the fruits of the blood of Christ." ... It "has purchased life, love, favor, grace, blessing, and whatsoever is promised in the Scriptures to them that believe and obey God," and it was Christ's blood that "stands between us and wrath, vengeance, curse."[11]

---

11 Tyndale, as quoted by Moynahan, 84. The spelling in this quotation has been modernized by this author in order to help today's reader.

Corrections and Distribution

Tyndale was aware that his New Testament, as a long-term project, would require future revisions. In reviewing the 1525 Cologne edition, he had already discovered seventy-two errors that required correction in his 1526 Worms edition. Like an artist scrutinizing every brush stroke of his masterpiece, Tyndale was a consummate perfectionist, always striving to make his translation the best it could be.

Other translation errors in the 1526 edition would be discovered and later corrected. Tyndale would make these adjustments in his 1534 and 1535 editions. In fact, he would make approximately four thousand corrections in these future editions. Some scholars have set the number as high as five thousand changes and corrections.[12] Most of these are slight adjustments, though a few are significant.

When the Worms edition of Tyndale's New Testament was printed, it was ready to be shipped abroad. Some of the newly printed pages were left unbound as loose sheets. Other pages were bound at Worms. Both versions were carefully hidden in bales of cotton to shield them from the eyes of government inspectors. These bales were loaded onto barges and floated up the Rhine River to a North Sea port. The cotton bales were transferred onto merchant ships to sail for the British Isles. These ships traveled trade routes from the European Continent to England to deliver their precious cargo. British shipping docks were ready to receive these valuable treasures. Most strategic among these ports was the grandest city of England: London. Other ships carried these newly printed Bibles to smaller ports along the southeast English coast. Some ships containing Tyndale's

---

12 Moynahan, 297.

Bibles sailed as far north as Scotland. The knowledge of the Word was spreading across the English-speaking world.

From these ports, Tyndale's New Testament was distributed to the major cities of the British Isles. Eager buyers purchased all the copies that were shipped. None remained unsold. The whole spectrum of English society had the Bible available to them in their own language. The two major English universities, Oxford and Cambridge, received copies of this banned book. Yet, it was the common man who mainly purchased these copies. People from all walks of life bought Tyndale's New Testament, including landowners, farmers, tailors, attorneys, carpenters, bricklayers, tinkers, professors, students, weavers, blacksmiths, and more.

The cost of purchasing one of Tyndale's Bibles was relatively low. When compared with other similar-sized books, the larger print run of this New Testament kept the price affordable. This allowed ordinary people to purchase their own copy. The cost was approximately half a week's wages for a common laborer. Farmers would offer a wagon of hay for a New Testament. Some people pooled resources in order to buy a copy to share. For the first time, a printed New Testament was available in England for those who could pay one shilling and eight pence for an unbound copy. A bound copy sold for a shilling extra.

Tyndale's dream was being realized. The plowboy in the field at last had the Word of God available to him.

Catholic Resistance

As Tyndale's Bibles were being distributed throughout England, the Catholic Church did not sit back idly. Alerted to Tyndale's scheme, the church in England began to purchase copies as it discovered them and to burn them on the streets of England. The church leaders in England feared an uprising by the people similar to the one in Germany, having witnessed the part played by Luther's Bible in the Peasants' War.

Cuthbert Tunstall, bishop of London, in October 1526 issued a prohibition against anyone so much as owning a Tyndale Bible. F.F. Bruce describes Tunstall as "specially disturbed by the importation and distribution of Tyndale's New Testament because naturally his diocese was more affected than anywhere else in the country."[13] Tunstall labeled these Bibles as "pestiferous" and a "most pernicious poison." Booksellers in England were threatened with imprisonment and death if they carried the banned book.

On October 26, 1526, Tunstall arranged for a public burning of Tyndale's New Testament at the famous St. Paul's Cathedral. Before the gathered crowd, Tunstall claimed to have found two thousand mistakes in Tyndale's translation. Such a claim is not surprising, as Tyndale had translated his Bible from the original Greek language, and Tunstall had made his charge based upon his investigation using the Latin Vulgate. Tyndale's English translation was far superior to Tunstall's inferior version. The two thousand mistakes were in Tunstall's Bible, not Tyndale's. Tyndale quipped that he was pleased that Tunstall had studied the Bible, even if it was to look for errors in his translation.

This strong resistance by the Catholic Church was but a harbinger of what would eventually come for Tyndale. Ten years later, this opposition would result in his martyrdom. For now, Bibles were burned. Later, it would be Tyndale who would be burned.

---

13 F.F. Bruce, *The English Bible: A History of Translations* (New York: Oxford University Press, 1961), 37.

Life as a Fugitive

The 1526 Worms print run is believed to have been either three thousand or six thousand copies, probably closer to three thousand. Out of this number, only three copies are known to exist in the twenty-first century. With these editions making their way across England, Tyndale's time in Worms was undoubtedly a success. But he did not remain there.

Tyndale's next known residence was Antwerp in the Low Countries. However, it is not until 1529 or early 1530 than he can be located there. Where was he in the interval between his time in Worms and his residence in Antwerp? And what was he doing during that period? Most scholars believe that he resided for a short time in Antwerp, and when he found that it was too dangerous to remain there, he returned to Hamburg, where he had resided before he went to Wittenberg and Cologne. In Hamburg, he took up residence again with Mrs. Emerson and continued his work of translation. However, there is no additional information concerning these events.

There is good reason to believe that after the Worms New Testament was printed, Tyndale turned his interests to the translation of the Old Testament. Tyndale had apparently translated a good portion of the books of Moses before he embarked on his voyage to Hamburg. On the voyage, his boat was shipwrecked and all of Tyndale's books and the translation he had completed were lost. This was a major setback to his attempt to translate the Bible into English.

However, this trial at sea would only impel Tyndale to persevere more in his mission to have the plowboy in the open fields of England know more of the Scripture than priests in the cathedrals of the churches of England. Regardless of whether Tyndale ever went to Hamburg again, the latter part of 1529 or early 1530 found him once again in Antwerp. This driven fugitive was ready to have the first five books of the Bible printed in the English language.

Tyndale was gripped with an ironclad fortitude to press forward in the face of numerous difficulties and hostilities. In the course of the Christian life, it is easy to so focus on our circumstances that we become discouraged and retreat or give up all together. Let us learn from the example of Tyndale's tenacious spirit not to give up, but to push ourselves to fulfill all God has sovereignly laid before our feet. For Tyndale, the most important matter at hand was to put the Bible in the hands of the people. Let us have the same drive to read, know, and digest the Word of God as Tyndale had to put it into our hands.

Father of Modern English

With his New Testament, Tyndale became the father of the Modern English language. He shaped the syntax, grammar, and vocabulary of the English language more than any man who ever lived—more than the author Geoffrey Chaucer, the playwright William Shakespeare, or the poets Percy Shelley and John Keats.

The English language at the dawn of the sixteenth century was crude and unrefined. It lacked precision and standardization, a strange mixture of Anglo-Saxon and Norman features with ancient Latin vocabulary, contained in disorganized syntax. Tyndale proved to be its change agent. As he translated the Bible, giving careful thought to words, phrases, and clauses, Tyndale shaped the language at its transition point from Middle English to Early Modern English. The speech of a nation was constructed in his mind and flowed from his pen. In providing the English Bible, Tyndale became the father of Modern English.

Moreover, Tyndale is recognized as the father of the English Bible. His influence upon how the English Bible would be written, read, studied, and preached reaches to this present hour. His translation became so foundational that until the twentieth century, every succeeding English translation was heavily dependent upon his labors. Eighty-four percent of the King James New Testament is a word-for-word copy of Tyndale's work. Of the Old Testament books that Tyndale translated, 76 percent of the King James is found in Tyndale.[14] Daniell notes that Tyndale wrote in "short Saxon sentences with largely Saxon vocabulary, a manner like proverbs."[15] In so doing, Tyndale translated the Bible into the vernacular of the people, which accounts for its widest possible audience and prolific influence throughout the English-speaking world.

Further, Tyndale is widely regarded as the father of the English Reformation. What most Reformers accomplished through preaching, Tyndale did by his Bible translation. Though he did preach during his younger years in England, in later years his full attention was set upon translating the Bible into the English language. Instead of proclaiming the Scripture, he gave the actual words of the Bible to Englishmen in their native tongue. If the people could read and understand the Word, he believed, God would kindle in their hearts a zeal for the truth. It was to this daring mission that Tyndale set himself, directing all his energies to this God-appointed task for the remainder of his life.

---

14 Moynahan, 402–3.
15 Daniell, introduction to William Tyndale, *Selected Writings*, vii.

5

Producing
the Pentateuch

William Tyndale saw the need of a fresh translation. . . .
Tyndale's vision was broader and more profound than Wycliffe's.
. . . Tyndale had a much better appreciation of what an English
translation of the Greek and Hebrew involved.[1]

—HUGHES OLIPHANT OLD

Indomitable in will and resolute in spirit, William Tyndale was never one to be slack when there was the work of God to be done. The need was too great. Tyndale was fully determined to translate the entire Bible into his native tongue, and nothing could divert him from this estimable task. He believed the work must be completed with haste, for his beloved homeland, shrouded in spiritual darkness, was in desperate need of the gospel of Christ. He was convinced that what he did had to be done urgently. Tyndale was undeniably

---

1 Hughes Oliphant Old, *The Reading and Preaching of the Scriptures in the Worship of the Christian Church, Vol. 4: The Age of the Reformation* (Grand Rapids, Mich.: Eerdmans, 2002), 137.

a Reformer not only in his doctrine, but in the propulsion and pace of his life.

Having revised and published the New Testament in 1526, this highly energized figure began the colossal challenge of translating the Old Testament into English. Given the greater length of the Law, the Prophets, and the Writings, combined with the greater difficulty of the Hebrew language, this would be a monumental undertaking for any translator. Such an enterprise had never before been attempted. It certainly had never been accomplished. Nevertheless, Tyndale was committed to giving the English people the entire Word of God in their own language. To this end, he gave himself relentlessly.

Several significant things were required for Tyndale to translate and publish the Old Testament. First, Tyndale would have to learn the difficult Hebrew language. Already proficient in seven languages, he now had to master this ancient Semitic language, which would be the most difficult and demanding of them all. Second, he would have to give attention to every verse, phrase, and word of the Hebrew Old Testament. Third, Tyndale would require a house in which to live and carry out his study and translation endeavor. He would again need several things he had needed for his New Testament project: a busy European city with a competent printer willing to assume the risk of being arrested and suffering the consequences; access to an ample supply of paper of significant quality; a location on a large river to allow for easy exporting to England; and an international business community that would allow him to disappear into the vast crowds of people when necessary.

Each of these critical components was provided in the city of Antwerp. Here, Tyndale would be able to advance to the next phase of his ambitious and daring project. Aware that the Old Testament would be more challenging than the New, Tyndale was ready to put his shoulder to this plow for this demanding assignment. The work would require scrupulous study, steadfast discipline, and unyielding drive. By the grace of God, Tyndale was ready for the challenge. This chapter will trace the steps Tyndale took in translating the first five books of the Old Testament, known as the Pentateuch.

Learning Hebrew

The first step in scaling this Mount Everest would be to learn Hebrew, a difficult language that does not resemble any of the seven he had previously learned. To the eye of an Englishman, Hebrew reads backward, moving right to left across the page. Words are based on a three-consonant root, and the basic forms are altered to produce related words. Vowels—not added to the written form until about the ninth century—take the form of dots around the consonants. These unique features posed a challenge for anyone trying to learn and work with this ancient language. Virtually no Hebrew was taught, studied, or known in England or the Holy Roman Empire at the time. No professor of Hebrew existed at any English university until 1524. There was no English context where Tyndale could have gained even an elementary knowledge of Hebrew vocabulary, verb forms, grammar, and syntax. Before departing for the European continent, Tyndale had no access to any form of Hebrew.

Upon arriving in Europe in 1524, Tyndale began learning Hebrew almost immediately. Becoming proficient in Hebrew in short order would have been well within his intellectual and linguistic capabilities. It is difficult to know precisely where, when, or how he learned the language, as Tyndale was living the life of an outlaw, so his wanderings and actions are shrouded in mystery. He kept no diary, wrote no letters, and preached no recorded sermons. No paper trail existed that could lead his enemies to his doorstep. He posed for no portrait, lest his likeness be recognized. His mission demanded that he remain an enigma. Consequently, Tyndale reveals little about the circumstances in which he attained proficiency in Hebrew.

The most plausible explanation is that Tyndale began acquiring the knowledge of Hebrew while in Wittenberg. Daniell explains, "Germany was the centre of what slender knowledge of Hebrew there was in Europe in the 1520s, and Tyndale clearly learned it there."[2] Historian Alister McGrath says Tyndale was drawn to Wittenberg like steel to a magnet because "Tyndale's heart lay with Luther's agenda."[3]

Luther had earlier taught himself Hebrew using Johannes Reuchlin's 1506 primer *De rudimentis hebraicis* (On the basics of Hebrew). Reuchlin was a master linguist who returned to Germany in order to perfect his Hebrew among the learned Jews living in the country. Reuchlin's grammar and dictionary became the first Hebrew text ever printed in Germany. It aided Luther in his translation of the Old Testament into German. As Tyndale would have conversed with Luther and read the German Reformer's translation of the Old Testament, Reuchlin's text then also played a significant role in Tyndale's learning Hebrew. Whatever instructed Luther in turn taught Tyndale.

---

2   David Daniell, introduction to *Tyndale's Old Testament*, ed. and with an introduction by David Daniell (New Haven, Conn.: Yale University Press, 1992), xvii.

3   McGrath, 70.

Translating Hebrew

Certain tools were necessary as Tyndale began his translation of the Old Testament. Like Luther before him, Tyndale would have needed Reuchlin's Hebrew textbook. He would also have purchased a Hebrew Old Testament from one of several German booksellers. However, Tyndale would have been unable to do comparative study with any extrabiblical Hebrew documents written during the time of the Old Testament, as none existed in the sixteenth century. The best he could do would be to consult works in other ancient Semitic languages, such as Arabic. Such resources would have been available to him in a local university, library, or monastery. He also utilized the volumes of an Aramaic commentary, the Complutensian Polyglot, and a paraphrase of the Old Testament in Aramaic.

In addition, Tyndale possessed a copy of Martin Luther's German translation of the Old Testament, printed a mere seven years earlier in the summer of 1523. Luther's translation of the Pentateuch from the Hebrew into German was the first of its kind. Luther also consulted numerous Hebrew sources that would have indirectly benefited Tyndale. Among these would have been the works of Franciscan Nicholas, Rashi, Pagnimus, Sebastian Munster, Bernard Zieglar, Matthew Aurogallus, and Andreas Osiander.[4]

Tyndale also had at his disposal the Old Testament expositions of another noted expositor, the Swiss Reformer Ulrich Zwingli. His sermons on the Pentateuch were in circulation by this time. These published discourses were based upon a meticulous study of the Hebrew text and would have provided Tyndale with further knowledge of this elusive language.

---

4   Daniell, *William Tyndale*, 298.

Providentially appearing in Antwerp a short time before Tyndale arrived was a French translation of the Old Testament by Jacques Lefevre, printed in 1528, which Tyndale no doubt consulted. Further, Tyndale would have also closely examined the Septuagint, the Greek translation of the Hebrew Bible produced one to two centuries before the time of Christ. Each of these tools made an enormous contribution to the work Tyndale was undertaking.

In translating the Old Testament, Tyndale developed his own distinctive style in accurately and clearly rendering the Hebrew into English. He sought to give the literal and plain sense of the Hebrew text in the English language in such a way that the common person could easily grasp its meaning. Wherever possible, Tyndale chose words of Anglo-Saxon origin rather than those of Latin or Norman derivation. Thus, he selected words such as *faith* instead of *fidelity*, *worship* over *adoration*, and *goodness* over *virtue*. Rather than using multisyllable words, Tyndale attempted to use one-syllable words whenever he could. For Tyndale, less is more in translation. This simplicity would aid the ease of reading and understanding for his audience.

An example of this is seen in Tyndale's translation of Exodus. His rendering of the Ten Commandments reads with familiar words that are easily understood:

> You shall have no other gods in My sight. . . . You shall make no graven image. . . . Remember the Sabbath that you sanctify it. . . . Honor your father and mother, that your days may be long. You shall not kill. You shall not break wedlock. You shall not steal. You shall bear no false witness against your neighbor. You shall not

covet your neighbor's house, neither shall you covet your neighbor's wife.[5]

In transferring the Pentateuch into English, Tyndale coined many English words, used for the first time, such as *Jehovah*,[6] *Passover*,[7] *scapegoat*,[8] *showbread*,[9] and *mercy seat*.[10] He also developed many phrases and sentences that have become commonplace in the English-speaking world. For example, in translating Exodus, Tyndale coined notable phrases such as an *eye for an eye, a tooth for a tooth*.[11] In handling the book of Numbers, Tyndale rendered the Hebrew in memorable fashion: The Lord bless you and keep you. The Lord make His face shine upon you and be merciful unto you. The Lord lift up His countenance upon you, and give you peace.[12]

Tyndale's translation style was consistent with his earlier work on the New Testament. For instance, he continued his practice of rendering possessive constructions with prepositional phrases; examples include *the fat of the land*,[13] *the beast of the field,* and *the law of the Lord*. With every word and phrase, Tyndale broke new ground in English linguistics, vocabulary, and grammar.

---

5 *Tyndale's Old Testament*, 116.
6 Ibid., 82.
7 Ibid., 106.
8 Ibid., 172.
9 Ibid., 582.
10 Ibid., xxii.
11 Ibid., 118.
12 Ibid., 209.
13 Tyndale, introduction to *Tyndale's Old Testament*, xxv.

Printing in Antwerp

Having learned Hebrew over a period of some five years, Tyndale was ready to begin the task of translating the books of the law. In late November or early December 1529, he sailed from Hamburg to Antwerp to oversee the initial printing of the Pentateuch. John Foxe records Tyndale in Hamburg working in close association with Miles Coverdale, translating the books of Moses, as early as 1529.

One possible reason Tyndale left Germany was an outbreak of life-threatening sweating sickness in Hamburg. But a more compelling reason for the move was that he would remain undiscovered by officials seeking to arrest and deport him back to England. His capture would have meant the end of the translation project and immediate death. A new location in a different city would enhance his ability to remain undetected.

During the sixteenth century, the city of Antwerp was located in the Seventeen Provinces (also known as Habsburg Netherlands) in the Holy Roman Empire. It would be Tyndale's base of operations for the next five years. With its waterfront access on the Scheldt River, Antwerp was the predominant port of Europe. As such, it was the greatest commercial city in northern Europe in the 1520s and the 1530s and enjoyed a period of wealth and advancement known as the Golden Age. It was so financially successful during this time that it came to be known simply as the Metropolis.

Being only nominally Catholic, its printers were willing to risk producing illegal Bibles for a profit. Likewise, its merchants were willing to transport the Bibles across the North Sea to the mouth of the Thames River. Upon his arrival in Antwerp, Tyndale moved into a boarding house known as the English House, located on a narrow street close to an enormous Catholic cathedral, whose spire rose above the other city buildings.

Tyndale selected an Antwerp printer named John Hoochstraten, who was a publisher, bookbinder, and bookseller. A government edict issued on December 7, 1530, made it illegal for anyone to write or print a new book without first securing letters of official approval. The penalty for such a violation would be "executed without delay or mercy."[14] An offender would be "marked with a red-hot iron," and his eyes would be plucked out of his head or his hands cut off.[15] Nevertheless, Hoochstraten accepted Tyndale's project and began the work.

In short order, Roman Catholic and local officials learned that a "heretic" was present in their city. Most likely, informants to the local archbishop discovered copies of Tyndale's Old Testament being smuggled onto ships in the harbor. On May 24, 1530, Archbishop of Canterbury William Warham issued a condemnation of Tyndale, citing "the translation of Scripture corrupted by William Tyndale, as well as in the Old Testament as in the New."[16] In June 1530, another proclamation was issued, identifying both the Old and New Testament translations of Tyndale as heretical works "now in print."[17]

Each of the five books of Moses translated by Tyndale was printed and published separately. The buyer could buy one book or purchase all five and bind them together. Each Mosaic book was printed individually so that they could be discreetly smuggled into England. A single book would be easier to conceal in a bale of cotton

---

14 Moynahan, 188.
15 Ibid.
16 Ibid., 190.
17 Ibid.

than five books printed as one large volume. Once these books reached England, the buyer could purchase them separately. Many English buyers then bound all five into a single work. Tyndale also wrote and printed each book with its own individual prologue.

To expedite the work, Hoochstraten kept two presses running simultaneously. This dual printing not only saved time but also reduced the printer's exposure to the crime of illegally publishing these banned books. Likewise, Tyndale lived in a state of urgency, desiring that the printed Word be available in England as swiftly as possible.

Genesis and Numbers were printed in the same roman type as the New Testament. Exodus was the only book that had illustrations with the biblical text. This second book of the law contained eleven full-page woodcuts. One picture was of Aaron dressed in the robes of a high priest, and the others showed the furnishings of the tabernacle. The woodcuts had previously been used two years earlier by another Antwerp printer, Willem Vosterman, who prepared them for a new Flemish Bible. Tyndale had limited financial means, and using these old woodcuts would have saved valuable resources.

Opening Prologues

At the beginning of his edition of the Pentateuch, Tyndale inserted an opening prologue that he had written as a general introduction to the five books of Moses. It is titled "W.T. to the Reader."[18] He explained how much opposition he had received for producing his English version of the New Testament. He references the claims by his opponents—that it was impossible to translate the Scriptures

---

18 *Tyndale's Old Testament*, 3.

into English with any accuracy, or that it was dangerous for lay-people to have an English Bible in their possession—and counters them in his prologue:

> When I had translated the New Testament, I added an epistle unto the latter end, in which I desired them that were learned to amend if ought were found amiss. But our malicious and wily hypocrites, which are so stubborn and hard-hearted in their wicked abominations, that it is not possible for them to amend any thing at all ... say, some of them, that it is impossible to translate the scripture into English; some, that it is not lawful for the lay-people to have it in their mother-tongue; some, that it would make them all heretics; as it would, no doubt, from many things which they of long time have falsely taught; and that is the whole cause wherefore they forbid it, though they other cloaks pretend: and some, or rather every one, say that it would make them rise against the king, whom they themselves (unto their damnation) never yet obeyed.[19]

Tyndale described his earlier travel to London as being for the purpose of securing permission from the bishop of London to translate the Bible into English:

> When I came before the chancellor, he threatened me grievously, and reviled me, and rated me as though I had been a dog. ... As I this thought, the bishop of London came to my remembrance, who Erasmus ... praiseth exceedingly, among other, in his Annotations on the new Testament, for his great learning. Then thought I, if I

---

19 Ibid.

might come to this man's service, I were happy. And so I gat me to London, and, through the acquaintance of my master, came to sir Harry Gilford, the king's grace's comptroller, and brought him an Oration of Isocrates, which I had translated out of Greek into English, and desired him to speak unto my lord of London for me.[20]

When the bishop of London refused permission, Tyndale realized there was nowhere in England to carry out his life's work. Therefore, he must travel abroad to do it. Tyndale comments, "There was no room in my lord of London's palace to translate the New Testament, but also . . . there was no place to do it in all England."[21]

Tyndale also placed a second prologue he had written at the beginning of the Pentateuch. This introduction was titled "A Prologue Showing the Use of the Scripture."[22] This prologue addresses the supreme importance of the Bible in the life of the believer. Tyndale compared the Bible to a precious jewel in the hand of one who did not know its true value. Tyndale further compared the Scripture to strong medicine that must be applied to every man's spiritual sores. He stated:

Though a man had a precious jewel and a rich, yet if he wist not the value thereof, nor wherefore it served, he were neither the better nor richer of a straw. Even so, though we read the scripture, and babble of it never so much, yet if we know not the use of it, and wherefore it was given, and what is therein to be sought, it profiteth us nothing at all. It is not enough, therefore, to read and talk of it only, but we must also desire God, day and night instantly, to

20 Ibid., 4.
21 Ibid., 5.
22 Ibid., 7.

open our eyes, and to make us understand and feel wherefore the
scripture was given, that we may apply the medicine of the scripture, every man to his own sores.[23]

Tyndale said the Bible was a light shining in a dark world that
alone can illuminate the way of travel for the believer:

> [T]he scripture is a light and sheweth us the true way, both what
> to do and what to hope. And a defence from all error, and a com-
> fort in adversity that we despair not, and feareth us in prosperity
> that we sin not.[24]

He urged the reader to consider every syllable of every word of
Scripture as being addressed to them directly from God Himself. No
matter how insignificant the text might seem, it is God speaking to
the reader:

> As thou readest, therefore, think that every syllable pertaineth to
> thine own self, and suck out the pith of the scripture, and arm
> thyself against all assaults.[25]

The Five Books of Moses

After the prologue to Genesis, Tyndale placed the text of the book
under the title "The First Book of Moses Called Genesis."[26] The text
begins in familiar fashion: "In the beginning God created heaven

---

23 Ibid.
24 Ibid.
25 Ibid., 8.
26 *Tyndale's Old Testament*, 15.

and earth. The earth was void and empty, and darkness was upon the deep, and the spirit of God moved upon the water."[27] There are no verse numbers, and the number of each chapter is spelled out. There are no cross-references, and the first explanatory note appears in the outside margin in Genesis 4. Incidentally, it is a comparison between Cain and the pope. There are only six marginal notes for the fifty chapters of Genesis, and of these, three are written against the Church of Rome. The explanatory note in Genesis 32 is of a more practical nature, addressing the subject of a believer's prayer.

The great majority of Tyndale's notes in the Pentateuch are explanatory, designed to explicate authorial intent and the meaning of the biblical text. Only a few notes are polemical, aimed at refuting Rome and the pope. Twenty-three notes are aimed at the pope, focusing upon the unfaithful conduct of the Roman church. Forty of the notes come directly from a book Tyndale had written earlier, *The Obedience of a Christian Man*. In the remainder of the Pentateuch, there are forty-six expository notes in Exodus, twenty-one in Leviticus, nineteen in Numbers, and forty-one in Deuteronomy. Most of these explanatory notes are relatively short. This makes a total of 126 marginal notes in Tyndale's Pentateuch.

After Genesis, Tyndale added a glossary of key words used in this first book of Moses. He called this list of words in Genesis and their definitions "A Table Expounding Certain Words."[28] This table functioned like a dictionary that defines words the reader might find difficult. He placed these key words in alphabetical order and explained the meaning of the words in simple terms. No English

27 Ibid.
28 Ibid., 81.

dictionary existed in the sixteenth century. Therefore, with this table, Tyndale became "the pioneer of English lexicography."[29] Here is a sampling of what Tyndale listed:

ARK. A ship made flat, as it were a chest or a coffer.

BLESS. God's blessings are His gifts.

CURSE. God's curse is the taking away of His benefits; as God cursed the earth, and made it barren. So now hunger, dearth, war, pestilence, and such like, are yet right curses, and signs of the wrath of God unto the unbelievers.

FIRMAMENT. The sky.

FAITH, is the believing of God's promises, and a sure trust in the goodness and truth of God: which faith justified Abraham, and was the mother of all his good works which he afterwards did.

GRACE. Favour: as Noah found grace; that is to say, found favour and love.

JEHOVAH, is God's name; neither is any creature so called; and it is as much to say as one that is of himself, and dependeth of nothing.

TESTAMENT, that is, an appointment made between God and man, and God's promises.

---

29 Moynahan, 199.

WALK. To walk with God is to live godly, and to walk in His commandments.[30]

A separate prologue was situated before the book of Exodus, titled "A Prologue into the Second Book of Moses Called Exodus."[31] The central idea of the book is explained as the believer's living out the truth of the Word of God. Tyndale states that the Scriptures have been given so that a believer may know "how to behave." Tyndale addressed the place of the law in the lives of Christians as guiding the pursuit of godliness. He announced that blessings or cursings follow the keeping or breaking of the law of Moses. In other words, Tyndale emphasized to his countrymen that the Scriptures they were reading for the first time in their own language must be learned by the reader, but also obeyed and lived out. He extolled the reader:

> Mayest thou understand how to behave thyself in this book also, and in all other books of the Scripture. Cleave unto the text and plain story, and endeavor thyself to search out the meaning of all that is described therein, and the true sense of all manner of speakings of the Scripture.[32]

As he did with Genesis, Tyndale included a table of key words in Exodus. He defined for the reader the meaning of basic words in his translation that he believed needed clarification. The following is a sampling from the Exodus list:

---

30 *Tyndale's Old Testament*, 81–83.
31 Ibid., 84.
32 Ibid.

CONSECRATE. To appoint a thing to holy uses.

DEDICATE. Purify or sanctify.

POLLUTE. Defile.

RECONCILE. To make at one, and to bring in grace or favour.

SANCTIFY. To cleanse and purify; to appoint a thing unto holy uses, and to separate from unclean and unholy uses.

WORSHIP. The bowing of a man's self upon the ground: as we ofttimes, as we kneel in our prayers, bow ourselves, and lie on our arms and hands, with our face to the ground.[33]

Appearing immediately after the biblical text of Exodus is "A Prologue into the Third Book of Moses Called Leviticus."[34] Tyndale described the place of the priestly sacrifices and ceremonies that were prescribed by God for those who worship Him. For a holy God may only be approached by sinful man only in the manner required by Him. He also issued a warning to the reader against allegorizing the true meaning of Scripture.

The ceremonies which are described in the book following were chiefly ordained of God (as I said in the end of the prologue upon Exodus), to occupy the minds of that people the Israelites, and to keep them from serving of God after the imagination of their

33 Tyndale, *Works,* 1:419.
34 *Tyndale's Old Testament,* 145.

own blind zeal and good intent; that their consciences might be stablished.[35]

Before the book of Numbers is "A Prologue into the Fourth Book of Moses Called Numbers."[36] This introduction is the longest of the five prologues in the Pentateuch. Tyndale concludes the prologue with this final exhortation to his readers: "Read God's word diligently and with a good heart and it shall teach you all things."[37] Concerning the law issued at Mount Sinai, Tyndale explained that the believer must practice it in his daily living. Tyndale laid great emphasis upon the necessity of personal obedience to the Word by the believer:

> In the second and third book they received the law; and in this fourth they begin to work and to practice. Of which practicing ye see many good ensamples of unbelief, and what free-will doth, when she taketh in hand to keep the law of her own power, without help of faith in the promises of God. . . . Now to be the son of God is to love God and His commandments, and to walk in His way, after the ensample of His Son Christ.[38]

The shortest of the five prologues in the Pentateuch is "A Prologue into the Fifth Book of Moses Called Deuteronomy."[39] Its

---

35 Ibid.
36 Ibid., 191.
37 Ibid., 198.
38 Ibid., 191.
39 Ibid., 254.

message calls for believers to have "love to God out of faith,"[40] which produces "the love of a man's neighbor."[41] This fifth prologue gives a brief synopsis of most of the chapters in Deuteronomy.

> This is a book worthy to be read in, day and night, and never to be out of hands: for it is the most excellent of all the books of Moses. It is easy also and light, and a very pure gospel, a preaching of faith and love: deducing the love to God out of faith, and the love of a man's neighbor out of the love of God. Herein also thou mayest learn right meditation or contemplation, which is nothing else save the calling to mind, and a repeating in the heart, of the glorious and wonderful deeds of God, and of His terrible handling of His enemies.[42]

At the end of the book, Tyndale includes a short glossary of terms he used throughout. Among these are:

> BELIAL, wicked or wickedness, he that hath cast the yoke of God off his neck and will not obey God.

> HORIMS, a kind of giants, and signifieth noble, because that of pride they called themselves nobles or gentles.

> ROCK, God is called a rock, because both he and his word lasteth ever.[43]

---

40 Ibid.
41 Ibid.
42 Ibid.
43 Ibid., 304–5.

A Monumental Achievement

Once his books were printed, Tyndale continued his practice of hiding them in bales of cotton in order to ship them to the British Isles. These copies of Scripture were smuggled undetected into England and Scotland.

During this time, all religious literature was written in Latin and all worship services were conducted in Latin, including Bible readings. The average person had little or no understanding of what was being said.

The English version of Tyndale's Pentateuch burst onto the scene as though it had been dropped out of heaven. Tyndale had translated the five books of Moses into English with remarkable plainness and clarity. The common Englishman could now easily understand the Word of God. The lucid style Tyndale used was energetic and engaging. He was succeeding in his goal of bringing the Scripture to the plowboy.

Tyndale's Pentateuch was the first portion of the Old Testament to be translated into English. Only a dozen or so copies have survived to this day. Most of these are complete, containing all five books of Moses bound together. One, in the Bodleian Library at Oxford, is of Genesis only. Another, in New York, contains Exodus–Deuteronomy.

In producing this first translation of the Pentateuch, Tyndale distinguished himself as a remarkable Hebrew scholar. Given the tools of his day, Tyndale's mastery of the Hebrew language was nothing short of astonishing. Tyndale performed his work at such a high level of excellence that some eighty years later when a team of scholars met to create the Authorized or King James Version, they could scarcely improve upon Tyndale's. In fact, Tyndale's translation was done at such a high level of proficiency that his work endures to the present hour through the many subsequent English translations it has influenced. Of all the gifts England has given to the world, none can surpass this masterful treasure. Wherever English is read, Tyndale's Bible is a priceless legacy.

Many paintings have been produced that represent the expansive influence of the British Empire around the world. One such painting, titled The Secret of England's Greatness, hangs in the National Portrait Gallery in London. In this famous work, painted in 1863 by Thomas Jones Baker, an African prince has sent an ambassador to Queen Victoria, monarch of England in the nineteenth century, asking the secret of England's superiority among the nations. The painting depicts the ambassador kneeling before the queen in the audience chamber at Windsor Castle. In the background are her husband, Prince Albert, and members of her court. Queen Victoria is handing a copy of the Bible to the humbled dignitary. The queen is silently saying, "Go tell your prince that this is the secret of England's political greatness."

The true greatness of England has been the English Bible. Over the past centuries, England has been a people of the Bible, and it has distributed that holy book's message to the four corners of the globe. The leading influence on this dissemination of biblical truth was the translation and publication work of William Tyndale. He was the first to present England with a Bible translated from the original Hebrew and Greek in their own language.

May the Word of God spread to the nations of the world in this day. May the sacrifice made by Tyndale five centuries ago be ever expanding in its influence in this hour.

6

Always Improving

Those former days of power, along with the truths
which then moved multitudes, all seemed forgotten amidst arid
academic theology and a modern evangelicalism which seemed
to know nothing of William Tyndale.[1]

—IAIN H. MURRAY

A s William Tyndale persevered in carrying out his daring mission, he did so as a marked man. He fulfilled this dangerous
work with his life in constant jeopardy. Repeatedly, government and
church-appointed agents were dispatched from England to scour the
European landscape in search of the fugitive. Multiple efforts had
been made to capture him by whatever means necessary. These emis-
saries were under strict orders to find Tyndale, arrest him, and bring
him to his execution. With his neck on the line and a price on his
head, Tyndale carried out his New Testament revision with a sense of
the high calling of God upon his life.

---

1 Iain H. Murray, *David Martyn Lloyd-Jones: The Fight of Faith, 1939–1981*
(Edinburgh, Scotland: Banner of Truth, 1990), 2:355.

After completing his initial translation of the 1526 New Testament, the Pentateuch in 1530, and Jonah in 1531, Tyndale refused to rest from his labors. He was steadfastly determined to revise his translation of the New Testament to improve its accuracy and readability. Exposed daily to the possibility of his own martyrdom, Tyndale was tenacious in pressing forward with the revision of his translation despite the danger of imminent capture.

When the 1526 New Testament was printed, Tyndale had already begun compiling a list of corrections he knew would eventually need to be made. In the postscript of the 1526 edition, he begged his readers for feedback regarding needed improvements for a revised translation. In 1534, eight and a half years after the first edition was published, Tyndale finished his tedious revision, which became his crowning achievement. New Testament scholar B.F. Westcott called this version his "noblest monument."[2] Tyndale expert David Daniell hailed it as "the glory of his life's work."[3]

A full decade after he arrived in Europe, Tyndale's Greek translation skills had been sharpened to a razor's edge. The 1534 edition underwent four thousand changes and corrections—five thousand, according to some scholars—a significant number and a remarkable improvement. The 1526 edition contained only the bare English text, a few explanatory notes, and a short epilogue. However, the 1534 edition contained the biblical text plus two general prologues, a prologue for each New Testament book except for Acts and Revelation, more explanatory notes, cross-references, and paragraph markings. At the conclusion of the New Testament, fifteen pages

2   Westcott, 141.
3   Daniell, *William Tyndale*, 319.

were added that listed and translated forty of the most important Old Testament passages.

The focus of this chapter is to investigate the tenacious spirit of William Tyndale and his arduous work on the 1534 New Testament. In the years before this edition was published, a challenge threatened the 1526 edition. At least four unauthorized versions appeared in circulation. These unsanctioned editions provided ferocious motivation for Tyndale to produce a corrected version of his original work. His revised 1534 New Testament proved to be the greatest of his works.

Unauthorized Editions

Almost immediately after the 1526 New Testament rolled off the printing press, unauthorized copies began to be printed and distributed throughout England. The printer most responsible for these pirated versions was an Antwerp publisher named Christopher Van Endhoven. No fewer than four unsanctioned editions came from his press without Tyndale's knowledge or permission. The first was produced in 1526–27, the second in 1530, the third in 1533, and the last in 1534. The 1534 edition would prove to be especially irksome to Tyndale thanks to the work of a man named George Joye.

A scholar from Cambridge who had become proficient in Latin, Joye performed editorial work on the last edition. Renounced as a heretic for his Reformed thinking, Joye left England and traveled to Antwerp, where he engaged in Bible translation of his own. He produced the first printed translation of several books of the Old Testament into English, though not from the original Hebrew.

In 1530, Joye produced his own printed translation of the Psalms from Latin into English. In 1531, Van Endhoven was arrested for printing and shipping copies of the English New Testament to England. He was sent to London when the authorities in Antwerp would not prosecute him, so he was imprisoned at Westminster and died there. In 1532, Joye published the translations of Proverbs and Ecclesiastes. In 1534, Jeremiah and Lamentations were translated into English from Latin.

In the spring of 1534, Van Endhoven's widow asked Joye to oversee editing on the fourth pirated edition of Tyndale's 1526 New Testament. The Flemish typesetters were struggling financially, and great profit was to be made in selling Tyndale's Bible. Joye made almost one hundred corrections to Tyndale's 1526 version, many of which were minor. Some of the changes were typographical corrections, while others proved to be significant. Joye's work was inferior to Tyndale's because he worked from the Vulgate to examine Tyndale's edition instead of the original Greek and Hebrew.

One unauthorized change in Joye's edition was a major deviation from Tyndale's theology. This created a firestorm of controversy. Joye altered Tyndale's word resurrection, changing it to the life after this life or very life in some twenty places. At the time, there was a brewing dispute among some of the Reformers about the idea of "soul sleep" as an intermediate state of the soul. Joye denied that a believer goes immediately into the presence of God after death.

These changes to Tyndale's translation adversely affected the public perception of his doctrinal stance. Tyndale denied this teaching and produced a second prologue to his 1534 New Testament accusing Joye of denying the bodily resurrection. Tyndale retained resurrection in the text of his new edition.

Printing Format

As he did with the Pentateuch four years earlier, Tyndale chose the bustling city of Antwerp to print and publish the 1534 New Testament. This busy commercial hub afforded him the advantages of a thriving business center with a number of English merchants. In this sixteenth-century metropolis, Tyndale easily remained undetected. Antwerp also possessed several printers from which Tyndale could choose for this important enterprise. Deviating from his chosen printer of the 1530 Pentateuch, Tyndale secured the services of a Frenchman named Martin de Keyser.

The revision was printed in the octavo format. It measured six inches tall, four inches wide, and one and a half inches thick. It was a stout, pocket-size volume small enough to fit in a hand. Though small in size, it was nevertheless a substantial volume of four hundred pages. This edition was printed in a blackletter typeface, rather than the roman type of Tyndale's previous translations, with a generous white border. The outside margins were an inch wide, containing multiple explanatory study notes and cross-references, and the top and bottom margins were spacious. The inside margins contained section letters indicating paragraph divisions. At the top of each page, the name of the particular book appeared, helping the reader find a specific text. Each chapter number was spelled out rather than being noted in Roman numerals. After all, Tyndale's primary audience was the merchants and farmers of England, not the learned scholars of universities.

Printing during the sixteenth century continued to advance with new technology. Printers would use a large sheet of paper folded one to five times, depending upon the desired size of the printed book. Each sheet would be printed on both sides. The simplest book to produce was the folio, which involved only one fold of the large sheet. This created two leaves printed front and back, producing four pages of text. A sheet folded twice was known as a quarto, making eight pages of text on four leaves. An octavo was a single sheet folded three times, producing sixteen pages of text on eight leaves. Tyndale chose the octavo format for its compact size, which allowed the owner to carry this forbidden Bible without its being noticed. This smaller version was also easier to hide in bales of cotton to be smuggled into England.

Title Page

The 1534 New Testament needed to be distinguished from the unauthorized editions of Tyndale's 1526 translation. To guard against any mistaken identity, Tyndale deviated from his earlier practice and included a title page that bore his full name. No ambiguity existed as to Tyndale's being the translator and editor. The full title page identified him as follows:

THE NEW TESTAMENT
diligently corrected and compared with the Greek
By
William Tyndale
and finished in the year of our Lord God
A. 1534
in the month of November[4]

---

4   *Tyndale's New Testament*, 1.

With its November 1534 date, this edition is sometimes referred to as the November New Testament. This nomenclature is similar to Martin Luther's 1522 German New Testament, known as the September Testament, because it was printed in September 1522. Though he identified himself as the translator, Tyndale chose to fabricate the publisher's name on the title page, which read, "Imprinted at Antwerp by Martin Emperor Anno 1534."

Opening Prologues

At the front of this 1534 edition, Tyndale first placed two introductory prologues that deal with the nature of his New Testament translation. The first prologue begins by identifying the translator and editor with the initials "W.T.," an unmistakable reference to William Tyndale. The prologue is titled "W.T. unto the Reader."[5] He carefully explains how this particular version is an improved edition in comparison with his earlier work. The first prologue begins as follows:

> Here thou hast, dear reader, the new Testament, or covenant made with us of God in Christ's blood, which I have looked over again, now at the last, with all diligence, and compared it unto the Greek, and have weeded out of it many faults, which lack of help at the beginning, and oversight, did sow therein.[6]

Tyndale also addressed the proper approach in translating from one language to another. He gave an explanation of his translation work with verb tenses from Greek into English:

---

5   Ibid., 3.
6   Tyndale, *Works,* 1:468.

If aught seem changed, or not altogether agreeing with the Greek, let the finder of the fault consider the Hebrew phrase or manner of speech, left in the Greek words; whose preterperfect tense and present tense are oft both one, and the future tense is the optative mood also, and the future tense oft the imperative mood in the active voice, and in the passive ever. Likewise person for person, number for number, and interrogation for a conditional, and such like, is with the Hebrews a common usage.[7]

Turning his attention to the subject of his explanatory notes set in the outside margins, Tyndale described their benefit in aiding the reader's understanding of a particular verse or to show its perceived relevance. He writes, "I have also in many places set light in the margin to understand the text by."[8] As in the first edition, Tyndale repeated his invitation for the readers to bring to his attention any corrections that needed to be amended.

If any man find faults either with the translation or aught beside (which is easier for many to do, than so well to have translated it themselves of their own pregnant wits at the beginning without an ensample) to the same it shall be lawful to translate it themselves, and to put what they lust thereto. If I shall perceive, either by myself or by information of other, that aught be escaped me, or might more plainly be translated, I will shortly after cause it to be amended.[9]

---

7   Ibid.
8   Ibid.
9   Ibid.

Tyndale did not conclude the prologue without explicitly stating the true nature of the gospel. He wrote, "The Gospel is glad tidings of mercy and grace, and that our corrupt nature shall be healed again for Christ's sake and for the merits of His deservings only."[10] The gospel of grace is received exclusively by faith alone in Jesus Christ alone. Saving faith, he argued, is not a mere confession to a priest, but the complete commitment of one's life to Christ. He maintained:

> Confession, not in the priest's ear, (for that is but man's invention,) but to God in the heart, and before all the congregation of God; how that we be sinners and sinful, and that our whole nature is corrupt, and inclined to sin and all unrighteousness, and therefore evil, wicked, and damnable.[11]

In addition to the first prologue, Tyndale included a second prologue to the New Testament. It begins as follows: "William Tyndale, Yet Once More to the Christian Reader."[12] Identifying himself not merely by initials but by name, Tyndale was compelled to address the dishonest misrepresentation that George Joye had made in printing an unauthorized version. He explaind that he had never approved the many changes made by Joye. This preface was a "violent protest against Joye."[13] Tyndale asserted:

> George Joye had not used the office of an honest man, seeing he knew that I was in correcting it myself: neither did walk after the

10 *Tyndale's New Testament*, 8.
11 Tyndale, *Works,* 1:477.
12 *Tyndale's New Testament*, 13.
13 Mozley, 282–83.

rules of the love and softness which Christ, and his disciples teach us, how that we should do nothing of strife to move debate, or of vainglory or of covetousness ... when the printing of mine was almost finished, one brought me a copy and shewed me so many places, in such wise altered that I was astonied and wondered not a little what fury had driven him to make such change and to call it a diligent correction.[14]

At the heart of this controversy, Tyndale was constrained to clarify that the changes Joye had made in replacing *resurrection* with *life after this life* were blatantly dishonest:

> For throughout Matthew, Mark and Luke perpetually: and oft in the Acts, and sometime in John and also in the Hebrews, where he findeth this word resurrection, he changeth it into the life after this life, or very life, and such like, as one that abhorred the name of the resurrection. . . . But of this I challenge George Joye, that he did not put his own name thereto and call it rather his own translation: and that he playeth Bo Peep.[15]

Biographer J.F. Mozley was correct when he wrote, "Tyndale's chief complaint ... was that Joye had no right to impose his own interpretation upon Tyndale's New Testament and saddle his brother with renderings of which he strongly disapproved."[16] Tyndale desired to set the record straight where his theology was concerned. He

---

14 *Tyndale's New Testament*, 13.
15 Ibid.
16 Mozley, 282–83.

vehemently disagreed with the doctrinal idea of "soul sleep" and aimed to correct any misrepresentation in his current biblical revision.

In this edition, each New Testament book has its own prologue, with the exception of Acts and Revelation. Most of the books and prologues have illustrations at the head that vary in length. The epistle to Romans receives the lengthiest treatment, being nearly as long as the epistle itself. The other prologues are "mostly very short,"[17] about one page long.

The prologue to Paul's epistle to the Romans unmistakably establishes Tyndale as an able theologian and Bible commentator. He begins by providing a chapter-by-chapter survey for the essential message of the book of Romans and a doctrinal synopsis of the gospel. All sixteen chapters of Romans have individual summaries written by Tyndale:

> Forasmuch as this epistle is the principal and most excellent part of the new Testament and most pure evangelion, that is to say, glad tidings, and that we call gospel, and also is a light and a way unto the whole scripture; I think it meet that every Christian man not only know it, by rote and without the book, but also exercise himself therein evermore continually, as with the daily bread of the soul. No man verily can read it too oft, or study it too well; for the more it is studied, the easier it is; the more it is chewed, the pleasanter it is; and the more groundly it is searched, the preciouser things are found in it, so great treasure of spiritual things lieth hid therein.[18]

---

17 Ibid., 285.
18 *Tyndale's New Testament*, 207.

Consistent with Reformed doctrine, Tyndale boldly states that the power of the gospel is entirely sufficient to change human lives. Stressing the primacy of the gospel as clearly stated in divinely inspired Scripture, he asserts that the epistle to the Romans contains a life-giving message of transformation for all who read and obey its words. When the Word is preached and received by faith, it sets free those imprisoned by Satan in darkness: "As we believe the glad tidings preached to us, the Holy Ghost entereth into our hearts, and looseth the bonds of the devil, which before possessed our hearts in captivity, and held them."[19] The faith that is required to believe the gospel is an active and living faith that trusts God entirely. Consequently, true faith leads one to commit his life to Jesus Christ. According to Tyndale, the result of genuine faith in the heart is abounding joy:

> Faith is, then, a lively and a stedfast trust in the favour of God, wherewith we commit ourselves altogether unto God; and that trust is so surely grounded, and sticketh so fast in our hearts, that a man would not once doubt of it, though he should die a thousand times therefor. And such trust, wrought by the Holy Ghost through faith, maketh a man glad, lusty, cheerful, and true-hearted unto God and unto all creatures.[20]

Translation Work

The most important part of Tyndale's revised New Testament is his meticulous translation work. Tyndale biographer J.F. Mozley writes, "The chief glory of the second New Testament lies not in its

---

19 Tyndale, *Works,* 1:488.
20 Ibid., 1:493.

accessories, but in the text itself. This was thoroughly and carefully revised."[21] Tyndale's proficiency in translating the Greek into English displayed his brilliance. Almost nine years after the 1526 translation, Tyndale's understanding of the Greek language had steadily advanced and matured. While studying Hebrew between 1526 and 1530, he nevertheless continued to craft his abilities in Greek. Daniell writes that Tyndale's knowledge of Hebrew gave him "insight into the Greek such as no other scholar or translator had at that time."[22]

Tyndale's linguistic expertise placed him "well ahead of any other scholar in Europe," Daniell notes, beyond "even the foremost professor of Greek, Philip Melanchthon at Wittenberg."[23] Tyndale operated at "a high level as a translator of Greek"[24] and was "a scholar of towering stature, leading all Europe in his knowledge of Greek."[25]

Commenting on the numerous changes Tyndale made in this edition, Westcott writes:

> Sometimes the changes are made to secure a closer accordance with the Greek: sometimes to gain a more vigorous or a more idiomatic rendering: sometimes to preserve a just uniformity: sometimes to introduce a new interpretation. The very minuteness of the changes he made is a singular testimony to the diligence with which Tindale still labored at his appointed work. Nothing seemed trifling to him.[26]

---

21 Mozley, 287.
22 Daniell, *William Tyndale*, 317.
23 Ibid., 318–19.
24 Ibid., 319.
25 Ibid.
26 Westcott, 144–45.

True to the text, Tyndale scrutinized each word and sifted out any Catholic terms that had been improperly translated into Latin. Such mistranslations carried centuries of theological baggage that twisted the true meaning of the text. For example, Tyndale replaced *church* with *congregation*. He substituted *senior* (1526) and later *elder* (1534) for *priest*. He chose *repent* for *do penance* and *acknowledge* for *confess*. These changes drastically undercut the false sacerdotalism of Rome that had prevailed for the previous thousand years. A genuine Reformer, Tyndale chose to be true to the biblical text despite the inevitable judgment of Rome.

The enduring influence of Tyndale's work can be seen in the many familiar phrases he crafted. Among these are *lead us not into temptation but deliver us from evil; knock and it shall be opened unto you; twinkling of an eye; a moment in time; seek and you shall find; judge not that you not be judged; let there be light; the powers that be; my brother's keeper; the salt of the earth; a law unto themselves; filthy lucre; it came to pass; gave up the ghost; the signs of the times; the spirit is willing; live and move and have our being; and fight the good fight.* The adaptations of these phrases have become timeless expressions for English-speaking people down through the centuries.

Mozley notes examples of improvements made by Tyndale in the 1534 edition. The wording of the 1534 edition appears first, and the 1526 version follows in parentheses. The words changed are in italics. From the Gospels and Acts, the following are highlighted:

Matthew i. 18. Mary was *betrothed to* (*married unto*) Joseph.

Matthew v. 9. Blessed are the *peace makers* (*maintainers of peace*).

Matthew viii. 26. O ye *of* (*endued with*) little faith.

Matthew xi. 29. And ye shall find *rest* (*ease*) unto your souls.

Mark vii. 11. Corban, *which* (*that*) is: *That thou desirest of me to help thee with is given God.* (*Whatsoever thing I offer, that same doth profit thee.*)

John i. i. In the beginning was *the* (*that*) word, and *the* (*that*) word was with God, and *the word was God* (*God was that word*).

John xx. 27. Be not *faithless but believing* (*without faith but believe*).

Acts vii. 60. Lord, *lay not this sin to their charge* (*impute not this sin unto them*).

Acts xix. 27. But *also that* (*that also*) the temple of the great *goddess* (omit *goddess*) Diana should be despised, and her *magnificence* (*majesty*) should be destroyed.[27]

As Tyndale revised, he made additional corrections to his work in the Epistles and Revelation. Again, the 1534 edition is written first, followed by the 1526 edition in parentheses. The italics indicate Tyndale's correction.

1 Corinthians v. 11. But now I *write* (*have written*) unto you.

---

27 As listed by Mozley, 287.

1 Corinthians xv. 51. I shew *you a mystery* (*a mystery unto you*).

Ephesians v. 19. Speaking unto yourselves in psalms and hymns and spiritual songs, singing and *making melody* (*playing*) to the Lord in your hearts.

Philippians ii. 12. *Work out* (*perform*) your own *salvation* (*health*) with fear and trembling.

Hebrews v. 7. Was also heard because *of his godliness* (*he had God in reverence*).

Hebrews xii. 16. Esau, which for one breakfast sold *his birth-right* (*his right that belonged unto him in that he was the eldest brother*).

Hebrews xiii. 14. For here have we no continuing city: but we seek *one* (*a city*) to come.

James v. 12. Let your *yea be yea and your nay nay* (*saying be yea yea, nay nay*).

1 Peter ii. 19. For it is *thankworthy* (*cometh of grace*), if a man for conscience toward God endure grief suffering wrongfully.

Revelation xiii. 5. Power was given unto him to *do* (*continue*) forty-two months.[28]

---

28 As listed by Mozley, 287–88.

In literary form, Tyndale's translation into English produced a beautiful prosaic style. His use of the English language departed from the highly formal manners of medieval expression, for this old genre was too stilted for the common man to read with clarity, understanding, or pleasure. Instead, Tyndale's translation technique produced a plain, readable, and straightforward text that was majestic in its wording and phrasing, yet easily understandable. As he had stated earlier, it was a book for the plowboy.

Marginal Notes

One distinct feature of the 1534 edition was the addition of explanatory notes in the outside margins. The 1526 version did not contain any side notes. In explaining a verse, Tyndale considered the larger context of a passage. In alliance with other Reformers, he believed Scripture can only properly be understood in context. Some of the marginal notes have a theological focus and connect a doctrine with the larger framework of the whole canon of Scripture. This method is called the *analogia Scriptura*, or the analogy of Scripture. In other words, Scripture best interprets Scripture. Tyndale rejected the allegorical method of interpretation and instead chose to discover the plain meaning of Scripture. Below is a sampling of his marginal notes:

> Matthew xvi. 21. When aught is said or done that should move to pride [i.e. Peter's confession], he dasheth them in the teeth with his death and passion.[29]

---

29 *Tyndale's New Testament*, 42.

1 Corinthians vii. 26. If a man have the gift, chastity is good, the more quietly to serve God; for the married have oft much trouble: but if the mind of the chaste be cumbered with other world business, what helpeth it? And if the married be the more quiet-minded thereby, what hurteth it? Neither of itself is better than the other, or pleaseth God more than the other. Neither is outward circumcision or outward baptism worth a pin of themselves save that they put us in remembrance to keep the covenant made between us and God.[30]

2 Corinthians xi. 20. (For ye suffer, even if a man bring you into bondage, if a man devour you, etc.) Too much meekness and obedience is not allowed in the kingdom of God, but all must be according to knowledge.[31]

1 Thessalonians iv. 11. (Study to be quiet, and to meddle with your own business, and to work with your own hands.) A good lesson for monks and idle friars.[32]

1 Peter ii. 5. (A spiritual house, and an holy priesthood, for to offer up spiritual sacrifice, acceptable to God by Jesus Christ.) We be that church, and the obedience of the heart is the spiritual sacrifice. Bodily sacrifice must be offered to our neighbor; for if thou offerest it to God, thou makest a bodily idol of him.[33]

---

30 Ibid., 250.
31 Ibid., 271.
32 Ibid., 302.
33 Ibid., 328.

1 Peter iv. 8. (Love covereth the multitude of sins.) Hate maketh sin of every trifle, but love looketh not on small things, but suffereth all things.[34]

The 1534 notes are less polemical than those in Tyndale's earlier edition and less caustic than Luther's notes in his 1522 New Testament. Tyndale primarily chose to explain the biblical text and address matters of daily Christian living related to the specific passage. Tyndale affirmed core Reformed doctrines such as justification by faith and also maintained that true faith gives evidence in good works. He repeatedly exhorted the reader to obey and follow the Word.

1535 Edition

The new 1534 edition of Tyndale's New Testament sold out quickly when it arrived on the shores of England. Within one month of its publication in November 1534, the next edition was already being printed and offered for sale in early 1535. The Gospels were printed at the end of 1534 and the remainder of the New Testament at the beginning of 1535.

This 1535 New Testament edition contained two title pages, each with a different date. The first title page is dated 1534, when the Gospels were printed. The second title page is dated 1535, when the rest of the books were printed. The title page of the latter edition reads, "The New Testament yet once again corrected by William Tyndale, 1535." In this edition, the initials "G.H." also appear on the title page. These stand for the publisher, Godfrey van der Haghen. Martin de Keyser was again the printer. In this version, Tyndale

---

34 Ibid., 330.

makes more corrections to the 1534 edition as he constantly sought faithfulness and accuracy to the text.

Tyndale made more than three hundred and fifty edits in his 1535 New Testament edition, most of them minor. He also made a few changes to his translation of the first five books of the Old Testament. He was continually fine-tuning his translation so that it would be the best it could be. Examples of these corrections are as follows:

John viii. 44. The lusts of your father ye will *do* (*follow*).

1 Corinthians xv. 10. I labored more abundantly than they all, *yet* (omit) not I.

Philippians ii. 4. *Look not every man on his own things, but every man on the things of other men* (1535). And that *no man consider his own, but what is meet for other* (1534).

Hebrews ix. 22. Without *shedding* (*effusion*) of blood is not remission.

James i. 27. To visit the *fatherless* (*friendless*) and widows in their adversity.[35]

This 1535 edition proved to be Tyndale's final revision of the New Testament. Only four copies of this third version exist today. Each is less than perfect, and only one still possesses the first title page, identifying it as the work of Tyndale. John Rogers used the

35 As listed by Mozley, 291–92.

1535 edition to compile his Matthew Bible. As a result, it is this latter edition that has become "the foundation of our standard English version."[36]

This period of tremendous productivity for Tyndale was quickly coming to a end. He would not see another edition of his New Testament, nor would he see his translation of the Old Testament Historical Books published. Within three months, this faithful servant would be arrested and thrown into prison. There would be no release from this imprisonment. After a year and a half of confinement, Tyndale would walk to the stake of martyrdom.

---

36 Mozley, 292.

The Historical Books

William Tyndale's Bible translations have been
the best-kept secrets in English Bible history.
Many people have heard of Tyndale: very few have read him.
Yet no other Englishman—not even Shakespeare—
has reached so many.[1]

—DAVID DANIELL

With his face set like flint toward the goal of bringing the Word of God to the English people, William Tyndale pressed forward continually in the work of God. The adversity he faced was daunting, and the dangers he encountered were life-threatening. Nevertheless, as a man of remarkable perseverance, Tyndale endured in his mission. Resolute in his labors, Tyndale would never cease until he had translated the entire Bible into English and it was placed into the hands of the plowboy in his beloved homeland. With stubborn tenacity, Tyndale could not be stopped until the hangman's noose strangled him and fire consumed him.

---

1 Daniell, introduction to *Tyndale's New Testament*, vii.

A life of greatness is most often marked by an indomitable spirit. Lesser individuals give up too easily when their path is blocked. But the one who leaves an indelible imprint upon the world is distinguished by single-minded determination in the face of rising censure and antagonism. Such a man was William Tyndale, a granite-like figure with imperturbable resolve.

Having translated only the first five books of the Old Testament (1536) and Jonah (1531), Tyndale had before him the vast frontier of the rest of the Old Testament, begging to be released from ancient obscurity. This included the Historical Books, the Poetical Books, and the rest of the Prophets. The focus of this chapter is the final work that Tyndale completed before his arrest and martyrdom.

Remaining in Antwerp

Having revised the third edition of the New Testament in 1534–35, Tyndale chose to remain in Antwerp to continue his translation work. As noted in the previous chapter, Antwerp had become the premier commercial center in Europe and had a sizeable population of English businessmen. The city's heavy traffic provided Tyndale with safe cover to guard his anonymity during his project, and its merchants provided the means to easily ship his works.

In this thriving city, there was a sufficient number of printers from whom Tyndale could choose. This strategic location provided the water access needed to transport the Bibles on ships in order that they could be smuggled into England. In addition, Tyndale had a familiarity with Antwerp that allowed him to continue to function with a degree of ease. For these reasons, Tyndale continued to base his operation in Antwerp.

Some English merchants who had relocated to Antwerp were sympathetic to the Reformed cause. One such businessman, Thomas Poyntz, provided housing for Tyndale in a boarding house known as the English House. Here Tyndale would find refuge and a quiet place to perform his translation work.

A merchant from North Ockendon, Poyntz and his wife graciously hosted Tyndale when he first came to Antwerp. The connection came through Lady Anne Walsh, to whom Thomas Poyntz was related and whose family Tyndale had served years earlier while in England on their estate, Little Sodbury. After leaving Cambridge, Tyndale had acted as chaplain and tutor to the Walsh family. Through Tyndale, Sir John and Lady Anne Walsh became convinced of Reformed doctrine and gave money to support and assist his efforts while he was in Europe.

During Tyndale's stay in the boarding house, Poyntz was a great help to him. Poyntz gave Tyndale a place to live and study in order to further sharpen his language skills and carry out his tedious translation work. The Poyntzes maintained his secrecy and gave him needed encouragement and counsel as his work progressed.

Historical Books

Tyndale never wavered from his goal to translate the rest of the Old Testament into English. Having completed the first five books of the Old Testament, along with Jonah, he devoted himself to translating the next eight books after the Pentateuch, starting with Joshua. He moved consecutively through this section of the Old Testament book by book, chapter by chapter, and verse by verse until he completed 2 Chronicles. This translation coincided with his revisions of the New Testament.

The Hebrew translation of the Historical Books proved to be a greater challenge than the translation of the Pentateuch due to the books' vocabulary and syntax. The book of Genesis had a limited Hebrew vocabulary and a rather elementary syntax, which made the translation work far less taxing, while the vocabulary of the Historical Books was much larger and its syntax far more demanding, which made it more difficult for Tyndale to translate them into understandable English. For instance, the books of Samuel and Kings frequently make use of rare Hebrew words, a tendency that presented Tyndale with difficulty in rendering the verses accurately and understandably for the average reader.

Tyndale also faced the challenge of translating the long lists contained in the Historical Books in a manner that would not lose the reader's interest and attention. When the same Hebrew word was used multiple times in the same context, Tyndale attempted to use alternate words in English to keep the cadence of the reader moving at a relatively quick stride. He believed synonyms helped in retaining the attention of the reader. For example, English literary scholar David Daniell points out that Tyndale translated the simple Hebrew preposition *tahtaw* in various ways, including "in his room," "in his stead," and "in his place."[2] Depending upon the context, Tyndale also rendered the Hebrew word *mahaloqet* as "number," "host," "part," or "company." The use of these alternate words provided variety and visual interest for the reader.

John Rogers

In 1534, as Tyndale unremittingly worked on his translation of the Historical Books, an Englishman named John Rogers arrived in Antwerp.

---

2   Daniell, *William Tyndale*, 339.

Born in 1500 and educated at Pembroke Hall, Cambridge, Rogers became a rector in the Catholic Church at Holy Trinity the Less in London. He then journeyed to Antwerp to become the chaplain to the English merchants of the Company of the Merchant Adventurers. This group was composed of English businessmen who lived together in the large boarding house of the Poyntz family. This residence provided a safe haven for its inhabitants, who were away from home. Religiously sympathetic, these businessmen pooled their resources and hired Rogers to serve as their chaplain while they were abroad.

Rogers moved into this new chaplaincy and quickly met Tyndale. Their relationship proved to be mutually beneficial. Tyndale became a strong spiritual influence upon Rogers and eventually led Rogers to grasp the saving grace of Christ and to convert to Protestantism. Whether Rogers was converted while with Tyndale or shortly after Tyndale's death is hard to determine. Nevertheless, through the influence of Tyndale, Rogers abandoned his Roman Catholic dogma and came to faith alone in Jesus Christ alone. As John Foxe records, Rogers at this time "threw off the heavy yoke of Popery."[3]

Rogers would play a critically important role in furthering Tyndale's life work of Bible translation. In 1537, Rogers published the entire body of Tyndale's translation work in what came to be known as the Matthew Bible. Hughes Oliphant Old comments, "Rogers was Tyndale's heir in regard to that most important work of Christian scholarship."[4] Rogers became the first martyr to perish under Bloody Mary, so "he was Tyndale's heir in martyrdom as well."[5]

---

3 John Foxe, *The Acts and Monuments of the Church: Containing the History and Sufferings of the Martyrs* (New York: Robert Carter & Brothers, 1855), 713.

4 Old, 138.

5 Ibid.

Tyndale Arrested

After translating Joshua through 2 Chronicles, Tyndale was arrested through the deception of a betrayer. An Englishman named Harry Phillips had arrived in Antwerp in early summer 1535 on assignment to find Tyndale and lead government and church officials to apprehend him. Phillips had previously lost a vast amount of his father's money in England and was desperate to recover the lost fortune. The Catholic Church seized upon his plight and offered to pay him a handsome reward in return for his assistance in apprehending Tyndale. Upon his arrival, Phillips made the necessary contacts that led him to the Poyntz boarding house. He quickly befriended Tyndale, winning his confidence and trust. Poyntz warned Tyndale about Phillips, but Tyndale remained naive to Phillips' clandestine tactics.

After he had completed his translation of the eight Historical Books, Tyndale lowered his guard with Phillips and became like a lamb led to the slaughter. On their way to dinner one evening, Tyndale and Phillips entered a narrow alley outside of the Poyntz boarding house. Phillips insisted that Tyndale walk ahead of him into the alley, where, by prearrangement, soldiers waited hidden from view on each side of a doorway. When he followed Tyndale through the door, Phillips pointed down at Tyndale to indicate that he was the person they were to ambush. The soldiers seized Tyndale and placed him under arrest. After being a fugitive for twelve years, he was now in the custody of the officials.

In this chaotic moment, Tyndale's room in the boarding house was ransacked and his possessions confiscated. Providentially, John Rogers had gathered Tyndale's unpublished work on Joshua through 2 Chronicles and escaped to safety. Rogers now had Tyndale's entire body of translation work in hand, including the entire New

Testament and his Old Testament work. In addition, he possessed Tyndale's prologues, marginal notes, and tables for each translated book. Tyndale was taken to the castle of Vilvoorde and imprisoned there for a year and a half. He was tied to a stake, strangled, and burned in 1536 for his efforts in translating the Word of God into the English language.

The Matthew Bible

In 1537, the year after Tyndale's martyrdom, John Rogers compiled, edited, and printed the Matthew Bible, so named because it was published under the pseudonym Thomas Matthew. Tyndale did not live to see the entirety of his translation work printed. Rogers took up Tyndale's mantle and published what his mentor had completed. Rogers was not the translator in this project, but instead acted as a general editor who collected and published this English version of the Bible with minor edits.

The Matthew Bible was the combined work of three individuals. This dynamic triad was William Tyndale, John Rogers, and Miles Coverdale. The entire New Testament was the singular work of Tyndale. His New Testament was first completely published in 1526 and subsequently revised and printed twice, in 1534 and 1535. The Pentateuch was also the exclusive work of Tyndale, first printed in 1530 then revised in 1535. The book of Jonah was probably translated by Tyndale and printed in 1531. Added to this were the books of Joshua through 2 Chronicles, translated by Tyndale in 1535. These books constitute the entire life's work of the inimitable William Tyndale.

Supplementing the work of Tyndale in the Matthew Bible was the Old Testament translation of a scholar he met while at Oxford, Miles Coverdale. This Englishman translated the entire Bible into

English and had it published as the Coverdale Bible one year before Tyndale's martyrdom in 1535. It was the first Bible ever printed in the English language containing both the Old and New Testaments. It was officially approved by Henry VIII and ordered to be spread "among all the people." However, Coverdale's translations were from the Latin and German, not from the original Hebrew and Greek, as was Tyndale's more scholarly and precise work.

In addition to Tyndale's translation of the Pentateuch, Joshua through 2 Chronicles, and Jonah, John Rogers compiled Coverdale's work for the remainder of his Old Testament. While in Hamburg, Coverdale had earlier served as a proofreading assistant to Tyndale as Tyndale translated the Pentateuch.

There are several key pieces of evidence pointing to the fact that the text of the Historical Books in the Matthew Bible came from the pen of William Tyndale.[6] Though Tyndale's name does not appear on the work, it nevertheless bears his linguistic fingerprints. His authorship can be verified in several ways.

One, the style of the English translation of the eight Old Testament books clearly reveals Tyndale's distinctive approach. There are certain translated words that are peculiar to Tyndale. For example, David Daniell points out that Tyndale uses "peremptory" and "pleading" interchangeably for the Hebrew word *na'*. Tyndale takes it as a request between people striving to express equality of status, as "a fellowship" (2 Kings 2).[7] This word is found in Tyndale's Pentateuch and in the Historical Books of the Matthew Bible,

---

6   Listed by Daniell, introduction to *Tyndale's Old Testament*, xxv–xxvi.
7   Listed by Daniell, introduction to *Tyndale's Old Testament*, xxv.

indicating that they are the work of the same translator. Also, the musical instrument denoted by the Hebrew word *toph* is faithfully translated by Coverdale in Ezra and the books that follow as "tabret." However, the same word is translated by Tyndale as "timbrel" in the Pentateuch. Likewise, this same word is found in Judges 11; 1 Samuel 10, 18; 2 Samuel 6; and 1 Chronicles 13. Many such words are used in both sections. This continuity points to Tyndale as the same translator.

Two, the one who translated Joshua through 2 Chronicles made noticeable attempts to be easily understood by the average reader. The same ease of accessibility found in Tyndale's Pentateuch is evident in the Historical Books of the Matthew Bible as well. A comparative reading of Tyndale and Coverdale reveals Tyndale's as the superior work in simplicity of reading, suggesting that the translator of the Pentateuch and the translator of the Historical Books in the Matthew Bible are one and the same.

Three, the Historical Books of the Matthew Bible exhibit the same desire for variation in word choice as Tyndale's Pentateuch. The same diverse words can be recognized in both the Pentateuch and the Historical Books of the Matthew Bible, indicating that the same translator was at work in both sections. At the same time, a few other Hebrew words are the same in both the Tyndale and Coverdale translations, such as "covenant."

Four, Tyndale's Pentateuch and the Historical Books of the Matthew Bible both use prepositional phrases to render possessives. Instead of translating a phrase as "God's word," for instance, the translator consistently uses the prepositional phrase "the word of the God." Daniell references other idiosyncratic phrasings such as "the fat of the land," "observed dismal days," and "open high mountains and on high hills and under every green tree."[8] This translation of prose unmistakably points to Tyndale.

Five, there are large initials found throughout the Matthew Bible. These letters were used to indicate the one responsible for its work. The introduction to the Matthew Bible features the initials "I.R." and "H.R." These stand for the authors of the introduction, John Rogers and Henricus Rex. Before the Prophets, there are the initials "R.G." and "E.W.," referring to Richard Grafton and Edward Whitchurch, the London printers who financed and distributed the volume. At the end of the Old Testament, there is "W.T.," which undoubtedly represents William Tyndale, probably indicating Tyndale as the larger contributor. This makes Tyndale the translator of half the Old Testament in the Matthew Bible.

In his *Chronicle* of 1548, historian Edward Hall adds the Historical Books to the list of Tyndale's works. Hall writes:

> William Tyndale otherwise called Hichyns. ... This man translated the New testament into English and first put it in Print, and likewise he translated the v. books of Moses, Josua, Judicum, Ruth, the books of the Kings and the books of Paralipomenon, Nehemias or the first of Esdras, the Prophet Jonas, and no more of the holy scripture.[9]

Hall mentions "the books of the Kings," which includes the books of 1 and 2 Samuel and 1 and 2 Kings. What Hall calls "the

---

8   Listed by Daniell, introduction to *Tyndale's Old Testament*, xxv.
9   Edward Hall, as quoted by Daniell, *William Tyndale*, 333.

books of Paralipomenon" points to 1 and 2 Chronicles. "Nehemias" incorporates both Ezra and Nehemiah. The only discrepancy in Hall's record is that these two books, Ezra and Nehemiah, were probably translated by Coverdale.

The result of this internal and external evidence substantiates the argument for identifying Tyndale as the translator of Joshua through 2 Chronicles in the Matthew Bible. This further solidifies the work of translation performed by William Tyndale in the Old Testament as truly stunning.

The printing of the Matthew Bible was accomplished in Europe, and when it was about half-completed, two London printers, Richard Grafton and Edward Whitchurch, joined the project and finished it. Grafton was later incarcerated in Fleet Prison and required to post an enormous bond, vowing that he would not print or sell any more Bibles until the king and bishops could agree on a translation— something that would never take place.

After the printing was completed in 1537, the Matthew Bible had a fate similar to Tyndale's before it, as it was hidden in bales of cotton or barrels and smuggled into England. This was a highly risky mission as officials in the east ports of England were watching continuously for such contraband. Anyone concealing an English Bible would be immediately charged with treason and made subject to capital punishment.

In this daring enterprise, shipments had to be made in the middle of the night. They often landed in or around the English cities of Purfleet or Dagenham, more than two hundred miles from Antwerp.

Tyndale's Legacy

William Tyndale was a noted linguist and philologist. S.M. Houghton writes, "Whichever of seven languages he spoke the hearer would suppose him to be speaking in his native tongue."[10] As a skilled linguistic scholar, Tyndale introduced many words into the English language. In short, Tyndale knew how ordinary people talked. Many of the words introduced by Tyndale have been mistakenly credited to other authors, particularly Miles Coverdale, William Shakespeare, the King James Bible, and others.

For example, the word *behold* is attributed to the Coverdale Bible, when in fact it first appears in Tyndale's 1526 New Testament (Matt. 1:20; 7:4; 8:29; 12:49; 18:10; 26:65; John 11:3; Rev. 21:5). Other words that find their genesis in Tyndale's linguistic skills include: *fig leaves* (Gen. 3), *birthright* (Gen. 25), *ingathering* (Ex. 34), *sin offering* (Lev. 4), *morning watch* (1 Sam. 2), *handbreadth* (1 Kings 7), *spoiler* (2 Kings 17), *swaddling clothes* (Luke 2), *slaughter* (Acts 9; Heb. 7; James 5), and *ministering* (Heb. 1).[11] In addition, there are numerous words that find their first usage in Tyndale's New Testament (1526–34), including: *apostleship, brotherly, busybody, castaway, chasten, dividing, fisherman, godly, holy place, intercession, Jehovah, justifier, live, log, mercy seat, Passover, scapegoat, taskmaster, unbeliever, viper,* and *zealous.*[12]

Biographer David Teems quotes Stephen Greenblatt as saying, "Without Tyndale's New Testament ... it is difficult to imagine

---

10 S.M. Houghton, *Sketches from Church History* (Edinburgh, Scotland: Banner of Truth, 2001), 120.
11 David Teems, *Tyndale: The Man Who Gave God an English Voice* (Nashville, Tenn.: Thomas Nelson, 2012), 268.
12 Ibid., 269–70.

William Shakespeare the playwright."[13] Even Shakespeare must concede that he is an heir to this grand translator of the Scriptures. Repeatedly, Shakespeare uses words and phrases that he has obviously adopted from Tyndale's New Testament. For example, in *A Midsummer Night's Dream*, Shakespeare writes, "The eye of man hath not heard, the ear of man hath not seen, man's hand is not able to taste, his tongue to conceive, nor his heart to report, what my dream was." Tyndale's translation of 1 Corinthians 2:9 in the 1526 edition of his New Testament reads, "The eye hath not seen, and the ear hath not heard, neither hath entered into the heart of man, the things which God hath prepared for them that love Him."[14] The common usage of Tyndale throughout the Shakespearean canon is unmistakable. Again and again, Tyndale proves himself to be the father of the Modern English language.

The work of Tyndale was spreading like wildfire throughout England and abroad. At last, the English people had access to the Word of God in their native tongue. Countless multitudes from the sixteenth century to the modern day have benefited from the unceasing efforts of this paramount Bible translator. Even after his martyrdom, the work of William Tyndale would change the trajectory of modern civilization. The light of God's truth was breaking through the thick cloak of darkness to shine in every marketplace, field, and home in England.

---

13 Ibid., xxii.
14 Ibid., xxi.

Conclusion

We Want
Again Tyndales!

*[Tyndale] is like a man sending messages in war,
and sending the same message often because it is a chance
if any one runner will get through. . . . [Tyndale] was directly
or indirectly devoted to the same purpose: to circulate
the "gospel" either by comment or translation.*[1]

—C.S. LEWIS

Tyndale's final words before the chain around his neck strangled him to death were, "Lord, open the king of England's eyes." That dying prayer was answered two years after Tyndale's death, when King Henry VIII ordered that the Bible of Miles Coverdale was to be used in every parish in the land. The Coverdale Bible was largely based on Tyndale's work. Then, in 1539, Tyndale's own edition of the Bible became officially approved for printing.

Tyndale's translation inspired the great translations that followed,

---

1   C.S. Lewis, *English Literature in the Sixteenth Century* (New York: Oxford University Press, 1954), 182.

including the Great Bible (1539, also compiled by Coverdale), the Geneva Bible (1560), the Bishops' Bible (1568), the Douay-Rheims Bible (1582–1609), and the Authorized or King James Version (1611). A complete analysis of the King James shows that Tyndale's words account for eighty-four percent of the New Testament and more than seventy-five percent of the Old Testament. Many of the great modern English versions stand in the King James tradition and thus also draw inspiration from Tyndale, including the Revised Standard Version, the New American Standard Bible, and the English Standard Version.

The enormous debt owed by the English-speaking world to William Tyndale is incalculable. His crafting of the English language introduced new words into our vocabulary that are spoken every day in countries around the world. Ultimately, his work in translating the Bible from its original languages into the tongue of his homeland helped launch the English Reformation. The calling of God upon Tyndale's heart became a burning passion to see commoners read God's unadulterated Word. Unfortunately, most people have never heard of this man and his vast contribution has been greatly undervalued through the centuries.

We want again Tyndales to tenaciously face the insurmountable obstacles before them and overcome them with zealous resolve for the glory of God. We need Tyndales who translate the Bible into the languages of forgotten people groups around the world. We need Tyndales to proclaim the gospel through the written page in the face of imminent danger. We need Tyndales who passionately love the Word of God to fill every pulpit, every seminary, every Sunday School class, every lectern.

Let us learn to say with David—and no doubt with Tyndale— "How sweet are your words to my taste, sweeter than honey to my mouth!" (Ps. 119:103 ESV).

Bibliography

Bruce, F.F. *The English Bible: A History of Translations*. New York: Oxford University Press, 1961.

Daniell, David. Introduction to William Tyndale, *Selected Writings*. Edited and with an introduction by David Daniell. New York: Routledge, 2003.

———. Introduction to William Tyndale, *Tyndale's Old Testament*. Edited and with an introduction by David Daniell. New Haven, Conn.: Yale University Press, 1992.

———. *William Tyndale: A Biography*. New Haven, Conn.: Yale University Press, 1994.

D'Aubigné, J.H. Merle. *The Reformation in England*. 2 vols. 1878. Reprint, Edinburgh, Scotland: Banner of Truth, 1963.

Demaus, Robert, and Richard Lovett. *William Tyndale: A Biography*. London: The Religious Tract Society, 1886.

Edwards, Brian H. *God's Outlaw: The Story of William Tyndale and the English Bible*. Darlington, England: Evangelical, 1976.

Foxe, John. *Foxe's Book of Martyrs*. Nashville, Tenn.: Thomas Nelson, 2000.

———. *The Acts and Monuments of the Church: Containing the History and Sufferings of the Martyrs*. New York: Robert Carter & Brothers, 1855.

Houghton, S.M. *Sketches from Church History*. Edinburgh, Scotland: Banner of Truth, 1980.

Kenyon, Sir Frederick. *Our Bible and the Ancient Manuscripts: Being a History of the Text and Its Translations*. Whitefish, Mont.: Kessinger, 2007.

Kuiper, B.K. *The Church in History*. Grand Rapids, Mich.: Eerdmans, 1951.

Lane, A.N.S. "William Tyndale," in *Biographical Dictionary of Evangelicals*, edited by Timothy Larsen. Downers Grove, Ill.: InterVarsity Press, 2003.

Lewis, C.S. *English Literature in the Sixteenth Century*. New York: Oxford University Press, 1954.

Luther, Martin. *Luther's Works*. Vol. 32. Edited by George W. Forell. Philadelphia: Fortress, 1958.

McClintock, John, and James Strong. "William Tyndale," in *Cyclopedia of Biblical, Theological, and Ecclesiastical Literature*. Vol. 10. 1867–87. Reprint, Grand Rapids, Mich.: Baker Academic, 1981.

McGrath, Alister E. *In the Beginning: The Story of the King James Bible and How It Changed a Nation, a Language, and a Culture*. New York: Doubleday, 2001.

McRae, William J. *A Book to Die For: A Practical Study Guide on How Our Bible Came to Us*. Toronto: Clements, 2002. Cited in Tony Lane, "A Man for All People: Introducing William Tyndale." *Christian History* 6, no. 4 (1987), 6–9.

Moynahan, Brian. *God's Bestseller: William Tyndale, Thomas More, and the Writing of the English Bible; A Story of Martyrdom and Betrayal*. New York: St. Martin's, 2003.

Mozley, J.F. *William Tyndale*. 1937. Reprint, Westport, Conn.: Greenwood, 1971.

Murray, Iain H. *David Martyn Lloyd-Jones: The Fight of Faith 1939–1981*. Vol. 2. Edinburgh, Scotland: Banner of Truth, 1990.

Needham, N.R. *2000 Years of Christ's Power, Part 3: Renaissance and Reformation*. London: Grace, 2004.

Old, Hughes Oliphant. *The Reading and Preaching of the Scriptures in the Worship of the Christian Church, Vol. 4: The Age of the Reformation*. Grand Rapids, Mich.: Eerdmans, 2002.

Piper, John. *Filling Up the Afflictions of Christ: The Cost of Bringing the Gospel to the Nations in the Lives of William Tyndale, Adoniram Judson, and John Paton*. Wheaton, Ill.: Crossway, 2009.

Ryken, Leland. *The Word of God in English: Criteria for Excellence in Bible Translation*. Wheaton, Ill.: Crossway, 2002.

Schaff, Philip. *History of the Christian Church*. 8 vols. 1888. Reprint, Peabody, Mass.: Hendrickson, 2006.

Sheehan, Robert. "William Tyndale's Legacy." *The Banner of Truth* 24 (February 2010), no. 557.

Teems, David. *Tyndale: The Man Who Gave God an English Voice*. Nashville, Tenn.: Thomas Nelson, 2012.

Tyndale, William. *An Answer to Sir Thomas More's Dialogue*. 1531. Reprint, Cambridge, England: The Parker Society, 1850.

———. *Tyndale's New Testament*. Edited and with an introduction by David Daniell. New Haven, Conn.: Yale University Press, 1989.

———. *Tyndale's Old Testament*. Edited and with an introduction by David Daniell. New Haven, Conn.: Yale University Press, 1992.

———. *The Works of William Tyndale*. 2 vols. 1848–50. Reprint, Edinburgh, Scotland: Banner of Truth, 2010.

Westcott, Brooke Foss. *A General View of the History of the English Bible*. New York: Macmillan, 1916.

Index

About the Author

Dr. Steven J. Lawson is president and founder of OnePassion, a ministry designed to equip biblical expositors to bring about a new reformation in the church. Dr. Lawson is teacher for The Institute for Expository Preaching in cities around the world. He is a teaching fellow for Ligonier Ministries and professor of preaching at The Master's Seminary, where he is dean of the doctor of ministry program. He also serves as a member of the board at both Ligonier and The Master's Seminary. In addition, he is the executive editor for *Expositor Magazine.*

Dr. Lawson served as a pastor for thirty-four years in Arkansas and Alabama. Most recently, he was senior pastor of Christ Fellowship Baptist Church in Mobile, Ala. He is a graduate of Texas Tech University (B.B.A.), Dallas Theological Seminary (Th.M.), and Reformed Theological Seminary (D.Min.).

Dr. Lawson is the author of more than two dozen books, including *New Life in Christ, The Moment of Truth, The Kind of Preaching God Blesses, The Heroic Boldness of Martin Luther, The Gospel Focus of Charles Spurgeon, Foundations of Grace, Pillars of Grace, Famine in the Land,* verse-by-verse commentaries on Psalms and Job for the Holman Old Testament Commentary series, and *Philippians for You* in the God's Word for You series. He also serves as editor of the Long Line of Godly Men Profiles series with Ligonier Ministries.

Dr. Lawson's books have been translated into many languages, including Russian, Italian, Portuguese, Spanish, German, Albanian,

Korean, and Indonesian. He has contributed articles to magazines and theological journals including *Tabletalk*, *Banner of Truth*, *The Master's Seminary Journal*, *The Southern Baptist Journal of Theology*, *Bibliotheca Sacra*, *Decision*, and *Discipleship Journal*.